UNBIASED
ISRAEL AND PALESTINE

The Struggle for Land, Identity, and Survival.

Ethan D. Clark

All rights reserved. No part of this publication may be reproduced, distributed, or transmitted in any form or by any means, including photocopying, recording, or other electronic or mechanical methods, without the prior written permission of the publisher, except in the case of brief quotations embodied in critical reviews and certain other noncommercial uses permitted by copyright law.

Disclaimer:

The content within this book is presented for informational and educational purposes. The views and opinions expressed herein are those of the author, based on years of experience and extensive research into the Israel-Palestine conflict. This work aims to provide a balanced and comprehensive overview of the historical and contemporary aspects of the conflict.

While every effort has been made to ensure the accuracy and reliability of the information, the dynamic and complex nature of the conflict means that perspectives and interpretations may vary. The historical events, political policies, and personal narratives included in this book are subject to different interpretations by scholars, political analysts, and those directly involved in the conflict.

This book does not endorse any specific political view or solution to the conflict. It acknowledges the deeply held beliefs and emotions on all sides and respects the sovereignty and rights of both the Israeli and Palestinian peoples. The author and publisher are not responsible for any misinterpretation or misuse of the information provided.

Readers are encouraged to consider the information in the context of the evolving nature of the conflict and to engage in further research and dialogue to form their own understanding of this complex and multifaceted issue. This book is a starting point for exploration and discussion, not an endpoint of understanding.

Copyright © By Ethan D. Clark, 2023.

Table of Contents

Preface..**8**

Introduction 10

   Overview of the Israel-Palestine Conflict..............10

   Geographic and Historical Context......................14

chapter 1: Ancient and Medieval History......**19**

   Ancient Israel and Judea..19

   Islamic and Ottoman Rule................................... 22

chapter 2: The Roots of the Modern Conflict 27

   The Balfour Declaration and British Mandate.....27

   Zionist Movement and Arab Nationalism 32

   Holocaust Impact and Jewish Immigration.........37

chapter 3: The Creation of Israel and Early Wars **42**

   The 1947 UN Partition Plan.................................. 42

   The 1948 War of Independence and Nakba..........47

   The Suez Crisis of 1956... 52

CHAPTER 4: The Six-Day War and its Aftermath **58**

Prelude to the 1967 War *58*

CHAPTER 5: The Yom Kippur War and Peace Efforts **74**

The 1973 War Explained *74*

Camp David Accords *79*

The Egypt-Israel Peace Treaty *84*

CHAPTER 6: The First Intifada and Oslo Accords **91**

Rise of the Palestinian Liberation Organization (PLO) *91*

The First Intifada (1987-1993) *96*

The Oslo Accords and their Impact *101*

CHAPTER 7: The Second Intifada and Continued Conflict **106**

Causes and Course of the Second Intifada *106*

The Separation Barrier and International Response *111*

Shifts in Israeli and Palestinian Leadership *115*

CHAPTER 8: The Gaza Strip: Disengagement and Hamas **121**

Israeli Disengagement from Gaza (2005) *121*

The Rise of Hamas and Internal Palestinian Conflict 125

Gaza Wars: 2008, 2012, 2014 129

CHAPTER 9: Recent Developments and Escalations 134

Trump's Jerusalem Decision and its Repercussions 134

The Abraham Accords 138

The 2021 Escalation and Ceasefire 142

chapter 10: The 2023 Conflict: A Turning Point 147

The October 2023 Conflict 147

The Course of the Conflict 150

International and Regional Responses 154

CHAPTER 11: The Humanitarian and Cultural Impact 159

The Refugee Crisis and Diaspora 159

Human Rights Concerns and International Law 163

Cultural and Societal Impact on Both Sides 168

CHAPTER 12: Attempts at Peace and Future Prospects **173**

Historical Peace Efforts and Failures *173*

Conclusion **177**

Reflections on the Long-Term Conflict *177*

The Path Forward: Possibilities and Uncertainties *182*

Appendix **187**

Chronology of Major Events *187*

Key Figures in the Conflict *191*

PREFACE

In this comprehensive history of the Israel-Palestine conflict, we delve into the intricate and often turbulent history of two peoples and a land that has been the focal point of political, religious, and cultural contention for over a century. This book aims to provide an unbiased and detailed chronicle of the events, figures, and turning points that have shaped this enduring conflict.

As a seasoned war reporter with decades of experience covering the Middle East, I have witnessed firsthand the human cost of this conflict. My approach in this book is to go beyond the mere recounting of events. Instead, I aim to bring to the forefront the stories of individuals and communities affected by this long-standing struggle, offering insights into their lives and aspirations amidst the turmoil.

The history is presented in a narrative format, weaving together the complex historical events, geopolitical shifts, and personal stories. It's a tale of two peoples bound by history, yet divided by visions of their future, each with legitimate claims and deeply rooted aspirations.

This book does not seek to take sides but rather to present a factual and empathetic account of a conflict that has shaped not only the Middle East but also global politics. It is an attempt to offer a clear understanding of the events that have led to the current situation and to provide a nuanced perspective on what the future might hold for both Israelis and Palestinians.

The journey through these pages is a journey through time — from the ancient roots of Jewish and Arab claims to the land, through the dramatic changes of the 20th and 21st centuries, to the tumultuous events of 2023. It is my hope that this book will serve as a resource for those seeking to understand the complexities of the Israel-Palestine conflict and as a testament to the resilience of the human spirit in the face of adversity.

INTRODUCTION

Overview of the Israel-Palestine Conflict

In the ancient, sun-baked land known to many as the Holy Land, a story of conflict and yearning unfolds across the centuries. This land, sacred to Jews, Christians, and Muslims alike, has been a crucible of history, where empires rose and fell, and peoples converged and clashed.

Fast forward to the 20th century, a time marked by seismic shifts. In the aftermath of the Holocaust, the world witnessed the birth of Israel in 1948, a sanctuary for Jews but a catastrophe – a Nakba – for the Palestinian Arabs. Wars erupted, first in 1948 and then repeatedly over the decades, as neighboring Arab states challenged Israel's right to exist, and the Palestinians longed for a homeland.

The Six-Day War of 1967 was a pivotal moment, changing the map and deepening the rift. Israel's victory brought the West Bank, Gaza Strip, and East Jerusalem under its control. Palestinians found themselves living under occupation. The Oslo Accords of the 1990s sparked hope for peace, but it was a fragile dream, shattered by waves of violence and mistrust.

The Palestinian uprisings, known as Intifadas, brought the conflict to the streets. Stones against tanks, suicide bombers against airstrikes – a grim dance of death and defiance. The world watched, often in horror, as peace seemed to slip further away with each act of violence.

Gaza, dense and desperate, became a flashpoint. The Israeli disengagement in 2005, followed by Hamas's takeover, set the stage for recurring conflicts. Rockets raining on Israeli towns, punitive blockades, and devastating military operations marked the years.

The shifting sands of Middle East politics, with the Arab Spring and changing allegiances, brought new dimensions to the conflict. International efforts to broker peace ebbed and flowed, often stumbling over the same stumbling blocks: settlements, refugees, security, and the status of Jerusalem.

The Trump administration's unconventional approach, recognizing Jerusalem as Israel's capital and fostering the Abraham Accords, rewrote some old scripts but left the core issues unresolved. The Accords brought normalization between Israel and several Arab states but left the Palestinians feeling sidelined.

In 2023, tensions reached a boiling point. Provocations in Jerusalem, the plight of Palestinians in Gaza, and the relentless push of settlements ignited a new round of hostilities. The region braced itself as rockets lit up the sky, and air raid sirens wailed, heralding a conflict that seemed as intractable as it was heartbreaking.

The story of Israel and Palestine is a tale of dreams and nightmares, hope persistently shadowed by despair. It's a history soaked in the blood of innocents and the tears of generations, a testament to the enduring human yearning for a place to call home, for dignity, for peace. Yet, the path to peace remains elusive, winding through a labyrinth of pain, memory, and unyielding claims to a land too sacred, too loved to easily share.

Geographic and Historical Context

Situated at the crossroads of continents, the land that lies between the Jordan River and the Mediterranean Sea is more than just a geographic entity; it's a tapestry woven with the threads of history, culture, and faith. This region, ancient and revered, has witnessed the footsteps of prophets and the march of empires, a crossroad for civilizations from the dawn of recorded time.

For millennia, this land, which encompasses modern-day Israel and the Palestinian territories, has been a mosaic of landscapes and peoples. From the verdant hills of Galilee in the north to the arid expanse of the Negev desert in the south, from the bustling streets of Jerusalem to the restless waves of the Mediterranean, each corner tells a story, each stone whispers a tale of the past.

Historically, this region, often referred to as the Levant, has been a melting pot of cultures and religions. Ancient Canaanites, Israelites, Philistines, Assyrians, Babylonians, Greeks, Romans, Byzantines, and Ottomans – they all left their mark here, building cities, temples, and monuments, many of which stand to this day as silent witnesses to the tumultuous history of the land.

Judaism, Christianity, and Islam – three of the world's major religions – have deep roots in this soil. Jerusalem, a city sacred to all three, is a symbol of both unity and division, a city where history is alive in every alleyway and every stone.

The Jewish connection to this land is ancient and profound, tied to biblical narratives and historical presence. For centuries, Jews faced persecution and displacement, culminating in the horrors of the Holocaust. The yearning for a safe homeland led to the Zionist movement, a call for the return to their ancestral land.

The Palestinian Arabs, with their own deep historical and cultural ties to the land, found their lives and aspirations upended by the forces of history that brought waves of Jewish immigrants to their shores. Their struggle for self-determination, for a state of their own, became entwined with the wider Arab-Israeli conflict.

The Balfour Declaration of 1917, the British Mandate, the UN Partition Plan of 1947, and the wars that followed reshaped the land and its people. The green line drawn in the aftermath of the 1948 Arab-Israeli war became more than a boundary; it became a symbol of division and conflict.

In this land, history is not just a subject of study; it's a living, breathing presence. Every hill and valley, every city and village has a story to tell, stories of faith and fury, of exile and return, of ancient glories and modern struggles. It's a land where the past is always present, where every stone and every tree is part of a narrative that is still being written, a narrative steeped in the sacred and the profane, in triumphs and tragedies, in unending quests for peace in the midst of unyielding conflict.

CHAPTER 1: ANCIENT AND MEDIEVAL HISTORY

Ancient Israel and Judea

In the ancient lands that now encompass Israel and Palestine, the saga of ancient Israel and Judea is a crucial chapter. This era marks the birth, prosperity, and eventual decline of the ancient Israelite and Judean kingdoms, shaping the religious and cultural foundations of the Jewish people.

The Emergence of Ancient Israel: Around the 13th century BCE, during the late Bronze Age, a group known as the Israelites began to establish themselves in the hill country, now recognized as the West Bank. The biblical narrative tells of an Exodus from Egypt under Moses's leadership, culminating in the Israelites' settlement in this land.

The United Monarchy's Glory: The 10th century BCE witnessed the peak of ancient Israel under the rule of Kings David and Solomon. David, celebrated as both warrior and monarch, declared Jerusalem the capital, bringing the sacred Ark of the Covenant into the city. His son, Solomon, erected the First Temple, which became the epicenter of Jewish religious life.

This era, often portrayed as a golden age, was characterized by the unification of the tribes and cultural flourishing. Under David and Solomon, the kingdom expanded its reach across the region, though the extent of its wealth and power as depicted in the scriptures remains a topic of scholarly debate.

Division and Conquest: The death of Solomon led to internal divisions, splitting the kingdom into the northern Kingdom of Israel and the southern Kingdom of Judah. Israel, with its capital in Samaria, endured until its conquest by the Assyrian Empire in 722 BCE.

This invasion led to the dispersion of the ten northern tribes, an event that deeply impacted Jewish history.

The Kingdom of Judah, with Jerusalem as its hub, continued until its downfall in 586 BCE at the hands of the Babylonians. The destruction of the First Temple and the Babylonian Exile of the Jewish elite were pivotal events, reshaping Jewish identity and faith.

The Exile and Return: The Babylonian Exile was a time of introspection and transformation for the Jewish people, leading to the compilation and editing of much of the Hebrew Bible. The Persian conquest of Babylon in 539 BCE by Cyrus the Great allowed the exiled Jews to return, rebuild the Temple, and initiate the Second Temple period.

This historical period set the stage for the narratives and religious customs that would sustain Jewish identity through the ensuing centuries of dispersion. The legacy of ancient Israel and Judea, with its kings, prophets, and enduring tales, became an integral part of Jewish heritage, echoing into the present day.

Islamic and Ottoman Rule

The history of the land encompassing modern-day Israel and Palestine has been profoundly shaped by periods of Islamic and Ottoman rule, each leaving an indelible mark on the region's cultural and religious landscape.

Islamic Conquest and Rule (7th-11th Centuries):

The Islamic conquest of the Levant in the 7th century marked a significant turning point. In 636 CE, Muslim armies defeated the Byzantine forces at the Battle of Yarmouk, paving the way for Islamic rule. Jerusalem, revered in Islam as the site of Prophet Muhammad's night journey and ascension to heaven, was captured in 637 CE.

Under the Umayyad and Abbasid Caliphates, the region experienced religious and cultural diversity, with Muslims, Christians, and Jews coexisting relatively peacefully. The construction of significant Islamic landmarks, like the Al-Aqsa Mosque and the Dome of the Rock in Jerusalem, highlighted the city's importance in Islam.

Crusades and Ayyubid Period (11th-13th Centuries):

The arrival of the Crusaders in the late 11th century disrupted this equilibrium. Jerusalem fell to the Crusaders in 1099, leading to the establishment of Christian states in the region and a period of conflict and shifting control.

Saladin's Ayyubid dynasty eventually reconquered Jerusalem in 1187, and the subsequent treaty in 1192 with Richard the Lionheart restored Muslim control while allowing Christians pilgrimage rights. The Ayyubids maintained a policy of tolerance towards Christians and Jews, preserving the multi-religious character of the region.

Mamluk Rule (13th-16th Centuries):

The Mamluks, a military class that seized power in Egypt, eventually extended their control over the Levant. Their rule from the 13th to the 16th century was marked by stability and the flourishing of trade and commerce. Mamluk architecture and cultural contributions further enriched the region's diverse heritage.

Ottoman Era (16th-20th Centuries):

The Ottoman Empire's conquest of the region in 1517 introduced a new phase of governance. The Ottomans reorganized the land into administrative units, with Jerusalem as a provincial capital. This era saw a reinforcement of the region's Islamic identity, but the Ottomans also acknowledged the historical significance of Christian and Jewish sites, maintaining a degree of religious pluralism.

Under Ottoman rule, the region remained relatively peaceful, though it faced challenges such as local revolts, administrative corruption, and economic difficulties. The late 19th century saw the beginning of Zionist immigration, responding to European anti-Semitism and the appeal of historic Jewish ties to the land, setting the stage for future conflicts in the 20th century.

The end of World War I and the subsequent collapse of the Ottoman Empire marked the close of Ottoman rule in the region, leading to British mandate governance and the eventual establishment of the State of Israel. The legacy of Islamic and Ottoman periods continues to influence the religious, cultural, and political dynamics of Israel and Palestine today.

CHAPTER 2: THE ROOTS OF THE MODERN CONFLICT

The Balfour Declaration and British Mandate

The Balfour Declaration and the subsequent British Mandate were pivotal events in the history of the Israel-Palestine conflict, setting the stage for much of the turmoil and contention that followed in the region.

The Balfour Declaration (1917): Issued on November 2, 1917, the Balfour Declaration was a letter from British Foreign Secretary Arthur James Balfour to Lord Rothschild, a leader of the British Jewish community. It stated the British government's support for the establishment of a "national home for the Jewish people" in Palestine, then part of the Ottoman Empire. This declaration was significant for several reasons:

1. **Support for Zionism**: The declaration was a major political endorsement of the Zionist movement, which advocated for the establishment of a Jewish homeland in Palestine in response to widespread anti-Semitism and the persecution of Jews in Europe.

2. **Contradictory Promises**: During World War I, Britain had made conflicting promises to both Arabs and Jews. To Arab leaders, Britain had promised independence for Arab lands under Ottoman rule in exchange for their support against the Ottoman Empire. The Balfour Declaration seemed to contradict these promises, sowing seeds of future conflict.

3. **Jewish Immigration**: The declaration encouraged Jewish immigration to Palestine, leading to a significant increase in the Jewish

population in the following decades. This influx was viewed with apprehension and hostility by the Arab majority.

British Mandate for Palestine (1920-1948): Following the defeat of the Ottoman Empire in World War I, the League of Nations granted Britain the mandate to govern Palestine. The British Mandate period was marked by significant developments:

1. **Administrative Control**: The British established administrative control over Palestine, implementing policies that would have long-lasting effects on the region.

2. **Rising Tensions**: The mandate period saw growing tensions between the Jewish and Arab populations. Jewish immigration continued, fueled by the rise of Nazism in Europe and the Holocaust. The Arab population saw this as a

threat to their majority status and land ownership.

3. **Arab Revolt**: The tensions culminated in the Arab Revolt of 1936-1939, a nationalist uprising against British rule and mass Jewish immigration. In response, the British imposed restrictions on Jewish immigration and land purchases, but these measures did little to quell the unrest.

4. **World War II and its Aftermath**: During World War II, the British sought Jewish support and temporarily eased some restrictions. After the war, the Holocaust's horrors and the plight of Jewish refugees intensified international support for a Jewish state.

5. **Partition Plan**: Unable to reconcile Jewish and Arab aspirations, Britain turned the problem over to the United Nations. In 1947, the

UN proposed a partition plan dividing Palestine into separate Jewish and Arab states. The plan was accepted by Jewish leaders but rejected by the Arab side.

6. **End of the Mandate**: The British Mandate officially ended on May 14, 1948, leading to the declaration of the State of Israel. This was immediately followed by the Arab-Israeli War of 1948, as neighboring Arab states invaded to prevent the establishment of Israel.

The Balfour Declaration and the British Mandate period were critical in shaping the modern Israel-Palestine conflict, laying the groundwork for the enduring national, territorial, and political disputes in the region.

Zionist Movement and Arab Nationalism

The interplay between Zionist Movement and Arab Nationalism fundamentally shaped the course of the Israel-Palestine conflict. These two ideologies, emerging in response to different historical and sociopolitical circumstances, eventually came into direct conflict over the land of Palestine.

Zionist Movement:

1. **Origins and Ideology**: Zionism emerged in late 19th-century Europe as a nationalist movement among Jews. At its core, it sought to establish a Jewish homeland in Palestine in response to widespread anti-Semitism and the lack of a national state for Jews. Theodor Herzl, often regarded as the father of modern political Zionism, was instrumental in promoting the idea through the World Zionist Organization.

2. **Jewish Immigration to Palestine**: Fueled by pogroms in Eastern Europe and later by the rise of Nazism, many Jews immigrated to Palestine. This immigration was seen as a practical implementation of Zionist goals and was facilitated by organizations that purchased land and established Jewish settlements.

3. **British Support and the Balfour Declaration**: The Balfour Declaration of 1917 and the subsequent British Mandate period provided a political boost to the Zionist movement, legitimizing its aspirations and enabling more systematic Jewish immigration and settlement.

Arab Nationalism:

1. **Emergence and Principles**: Arab Nationalism emerged in the late 19th and early 20th centuries, seeking to unite Arabic-

speaking peoples under the banner of a common identity and independence from Ottoman and European colonial rule. It was motivated by a desire for self-determination and governance based on Arab cultural and political ideals.

2. **Response to Zionism and Jewish Immigration**: The increasing Jewish immigration to Palestine, encouraged by the Zionist movement and supported by British policies, was viewed by the Arab population as a direct threat to their land, culture, and political aspirations. Arab Nationalism in Palestine became increasingly anti-Zionist.

3. **Rising Tensions and Conflict**: The interwar period saw escalating tensions between Jewish and Arab communities in Palestine. Major Arab revolts and riots occurred, notably in 1920, 1929, and the Arab Revolt of 1936-1939,

reflecting growing resentment against British colonialism and the Zionist movement.

Conflict and Convergence:

1. **Competing Nationalisms**: The Zionist aspiration for a Jewish homeland in Palestine clashed directly with the Arab Nationalist goal of an independent Arab state in the same territory. This clash was exacerbated by the political and demographic changes brought about by Jewish immigration and land acquisition.

2. **British Role**: The British Mandate authorities often found themselves in a precarious position, attempting to balance the contradictory promises made to both Jews and Arabs. This only served to deepen mistrust among both communities.

3. **International Dimension**: The conflict between Zionist and Arab nationalisms in Palestine attracted international attention and intervention, culminating in the UN's 1947 partition plan, which sought to create separate Jewish and Arab states. The plan, accepted by the Jewish leadership but rejected by the Arab side, led to the outbreak of the 1948 Arab-Israeli War.

The Zionist movement and Arab nationalism were both responses to the desires and needs of their respective communities. However, their incompatible goals regarding the future of Palestine set them on a collision course, forming the basis of a protracted and complex conflict that continues to this day.

Holocaust Impact and Jewish Immigration

The Holocaust had a profound impact on the trajectory of the Israel-Palestine conflict, particularly in the context of Jewish immigration. This tragic period in history not only underscored the necessity of a safe haven for Jews but also dramatically influenced international attitudes towards the Zionist movement and the establishment of a Jewish state.

Impact of the Holocaust:

1. **Jewish Persecution and the Holocaust**: The Holocaust, during which six million Jews were systematically murdered by the Nazi regime, highlighted the vulnerability of Jews in Europe. The sheer scale and brutality of the Holocaust demonstrated the dangers of anti-Semitism and the lack of a national homeland for Jews.

2. **Urgency for a Safe Haven**: The Holocaust intensified the call within the Jewish community for a secure and sovereign state. The Zionist movement, which had been advocating for a Jewish homeland, gained new urgency and support as a necessary response to the existential threats faced by Jews.

3. **Sympathy and International Support**: The horrors of the Holocaust elicited sympathy for the Jewish cause worldwide. This change in attitude influenced international opinion, leading many to support the idea of a Jewish state as a refuge for survivors of the Holocaust.

Jewish Immigration to Palestine:

1. **Post-War Immigration**: After World War II, thousands of Jewish survivors, with no homes to return to and facing continued anti-Semitism in Europe, sought to immigrate to Palestine.

British restrictions on Jewish immigration to Palestine, however, led to illegal immigration and confrontations with British authorities.

2. **Displaced Persons Camps and Immigration**: Many Holocaust survivors ended up in Displaced Persons Camps in Europe. The dire conditions and the desire to leave Europe led to increased pressure on the British government to allow more Jewish immigration to Palestine.

3. **International Pressure**: The plight of Jewish refugees and survivors of the Holocaust led to international pressure on the British to relax immigration restrictions. The U.S., in particular, pushed for increased Jewish immigration to Palestine as a humanitarian necessity.

Consequences for the Israel-Palestine Conflict:

1. **Demographic Changes**: The influx of Jewish immigrants changed the demographic landscape of Palestine, heightening tensions between Jewish and Arab communities. The increased Jewish presence bolstered the Zionist claim to the land but also intensified Arab fears and opposition.

2. **Political Developments**: The surge in Jewish immigration and the aftermath of the Holocaust played a critical role in shaping the United Nations' decision to propose the partition of Palestine into separate Jewish and Arab states in 1947.

3. **Formation of Israel**: The Holocaust and the subsequent increase in Jewish immigration were key factors leading to the declaration of the State of Israel in 1948. The establishment of Israel was seen by many Jews as a necessary

response to the Holocaust, providing a safe and sovereign homeland for Jews.

The Holocaust not only underscored the perilous position of Jews without a homeland but also generated international sympathy for the Zionist cause. The subsequent increase in Jewish immigration to Palestine was a direct response to the Holocaust, setting the stage for the creation of the State of Israel and further intensifying the Israel-Palestine conflict.

CHAPTER 3: THE CREATION OF ISRAEL AND EARLY WARS

The 1947 UN Partition Plan

The 1947 UN Partition Plan marked a pivotal moment in the history of the Israel-Palestine conflict. This plan, officially known as United Nations General Assembly Resolution 181, proposed the partition of the British Mandate of Palestine into two separate states, one Jewish and one Arab, with Jerusalem under international administration.

Background of the Plan:

1. **End of British Mandate**: The British government, struggling to maintain peace between Jewish and Arab populations and faced with increasing violence, turned the Palestine issue over to the United Nations in 1947.

2. **Increasing Tensions**: The post-World War II period saw heightened tensions in Palestine, exacerbated by the Holocaust and increased Jewish immigration, leading to growing conflict between Jewish and Arab communities.

The Partition Proposal:

1. **Division of Territory**: The plan proposed dividing the land into three entities: a Jewish state, an Arab state, and an international zone around Jerusalem. The proposed Jewish state included regions with a Jewish majority, while the Arab state was in regions with an Arab majority.

2. **Economic Union**: It envisaged an economic union between the two states, allowing for free movement of goods and services.

3. **Jerusalem**: Jerusalem was to be placed under international administration due to its religious significance to Jews, Christians, and Muslims.

Reactions to the Plan:

1. **Jewish Acceptance**: The Jewish Agency, representing the Jewish community in Palestine, accepted the plan, seeing it as a pathway to statehood and recognition.

2. **Arab Rejection**: The Arab Higher Committee and surrounding Arab nations rejected the plan, opposing the idea of a Jewish state and any partition that didn't reflect the demographic majority of Arabs in the entire territory.

3. **International Perspective**: The plan was seen by many international observers as a compromise solution to a complex problem, although it was criticized by some for not

adequately addressing the concerns and rights of the Palestinian Arab population.

Consequences:

1. **Civil War in Mandatory Palestine**: The plan's announcement led to the outbreak of civil war in Mandatory Palestine, with Jewish and Arab communities engaging in violent conflict.

2. **Path to Israeli Independence**: For the Jewish community, the plan laid the groundwork for the declaration of the State of Israel in May 1948.

3. **1948 Arab-Israeli War**: The rejection of the plan by Arab nations and the subsequent declaration of Israeli independence led to the 1948 Arab-Israeli War, involving neighboring Arab states.

Legacy:

1. **Enduring Conflict**: The plan's failure to achieve a peaceful resolution and the subsequent wars entrenched the ongoing conflict between Israel and the Palestinians.

2. **Refugee Crisis**: The war that followed the plan's rejection led to a significant refugee crisis, with hundreds of thousands of Palestinians displaced from their homes.

3. **Shaping Modern Middle East**: The 1947 UN Partition Plan and its aftermath played a crucial role in shaping the geopolitical landscape of the modern Middle East, setting the stage for decades of conflict and negotiations.

The 1947 UN Partition Plan was a significant but ultimately unsuccessful attempt to resolve the conflict between Jews and Arabs in Palestine. Its legacy is a complex tapestry of statehood, conflict, and enduring contention over land and national identity.

The 1948 War of Independence and Nakba

The 1948 War of Independence for Israelis, also known as the Nakba (Catastrophe) by Palestinians, is a defining moment in the long-standing conflict between Israel and Palestine. This conflict not only led to the establishment of the State of Israel but also to a major displacement of Palestinians.

Outbreak of the War:

1. **Declaration of the State of Israel**: On May 14, 1948, David Ben-Gurion declared the establishment of the State of Israel. This declaration came on the heels of the British Mandate's expiration and was in line with the UN Partition Plan.

2. **Arab Rejection and Invasion**: The immediate response from neighboring Arab states was to reject the declaration and to invade the newly formed state, leading to a full-scale war.

Major Phases of the War:

1. **Initial Conflict**: The initial phase of the war involved sporadic fighting between Jewish and Palestinian Arab communities, escalating rapidly after the UN Partition Plan announcement.

2. **Intervention by Arab States**: Following Israel's declaration of independence, armies from Egypt, Jordan, Syria, Lebanon, and Iraq invaded the territory of the former British Mandate.

Consequences for Israel:

1. **Establishment of Sovereignty**: Despite facing larger and better-equipped armies, Israel managed to not only survive but also expand its territory beyond the UN Partition Plan's recommendations.

2. **Military and Political Victory**: The war established Israel as a significant military force in the region and solidified its status as an independent state.

Impact on Palestinians - The Nakba:

1. **Displacement of Palestinians**: The war led to the displacement of approximately 700,000 Palestinian Arabs. This mass exodus was caused by a combination of factors including fear of violence, expulsion by Israeli forces, and the chaos of war.

2. **Loss of Homeland**: For Palestinians, the Nakba represents a profound loss - the loss of their homes and the denial of the right to return.

3. **Creation of the Refugee Crisis**: The displaced Palestinians ended up in refugee camps in neighboring countries, and the refugee issue remains one of the most contentious elements of the Israeli-Palestinian conflict.

Aftermath and International Reactions:

1. **Armistice Agreements**: In 1949, armistice agreements were signed between Israel and Egypt, Jordan, Lebanon, and Syria, establishing new borders, notably leaving the West Bank under Jordanian control and the Gaza Strip under Egyptian control.

2. **International Recognition**: Israel gained recognition from many countries post-war,

including the United States and the Soviet Union, solidifying its international status.

3. **Unresolved Issues**: The war left many issues unresolved, such as the status of Jerusalem, the borders of Israel, and the right of return for Palestinian refugees.

Long-term Effects:

1. **Ongoing Conflict**: The 1948 war set the stage for future conflicts in the region, including the 1967 Six-Day War and the continued Israeli-Palestinian conflict.

2. **Shaping National Identities**: The war significantly influenced the national identities of both Israelis and Palestinians, with each group viewing the war through vastly different lenses - victory and independence versus catastrophe and dispossession.

In summary, the 1948 War of Independence/Nakba is a central historical event that shaped the current dynamics of the Israeli-Palestinian conflict. It's a story of state formation, survival, and tragedy that has left a deep and lasting impact on the region and its peoples.

The Suez Crisis of 1956

The Suez Crisis of 1956, also known as the Tripartite Aggression or the Sinai Campaign, was a pivotal event in the history of the Middle East, marking a significant turning point in the post-World War II geopolitical landscape. This crisis involved Israel, Egypt, the United Kingdom, and France, and was centered around the control of the Suez Canal, a crucial waterway for international trade and military movements.

Background:

1. **Nationalization of the Suez Canal**: In July 1956, Egyptian President Gamal Abdel Nasser nationalized the Suez Canal, previously controlled by the British and French. This move was partly in response to the withdrawal of US and British funding for the Aswan Dam project.

2. **Strategic Importance**: The Canal was a vital maritime route for European powers, particularly for the shipment of oil from the Middle East.

Israel's Motivations and Objectives:

1. **Fedayeen Raids**: Israel faced continuous cross-border raids (Fedayeen attacks) from the Gaza Strip, which was under Egyptian control.

2. **Strategic Security**: Israel sought to improve its strategic security position by weakening Egypt's military capabilities.

3. **Navigation Rights**: Israel was also concerned about Egypt's blockade of the Straits of Tiran, which restricted Israeli shipping.

The Tripartite Plan:

1. **Secret Agreement**: The United Kingdom and France, seeking to regain control over the Suez Canal and to curtail Nasser's growing influence, entered into a secret agreement with Israel.

2. **Military Campaign**: Under the plan, Israel would invade the Sinai Peninsula, followed by an Anglo-French intervention purportedly to separate the combatants and safeguard the Canal.

The Conflict:

1. **Israeli Invasion**: In late October 1956, Israel launched a successful military campaign against Egypt in the Sinai Peninsula.

2. **Anglo-French Intervention**: Following the Israeli advance, British and French forces issued an ultimatum and then commenced aerial and naval bombardments before conducting a limited landing.

International Response:

1. **United States and Soviet Union**: Both superpowers, the United States and the Soviet Union, opposed the invasion. The Eisenhower administration exerted significant economic and diplomatic pressure on Britain, France, and Israel to withdraw.

2. **United Nations**: The crisis led to the first-ever emergency special session of the UN General Assembly and the creation of the United Nations Emergency Force (UNEF) to facilitate the withdrawal of invading forces and to stabilize the situation.

Aftermath and Consequences:

1. **Withdrawal**: By March 1957, Israel, Britain, and France had withdrawn their forces under international pressure.

2. **Nasser's Prestige**: Nasser emerged from the crisis with his prestige in the Arab world significantly enhanced, having withstood the assault by two European powers and Israel.

3. **British and French Decline**: The crisis marked the end of Britain and France's role as major players in the Middle East.

4. **UN Peacekeeping**: The deployment of UNEF set a precedent for future United Nations peacekeeping missions.

5. **Shift in Global Power**: The crisis illustrated the shift in global power away from the old

European colonial powers to the US-Soviet bipolar world order of the Cold War era.

The Suez Crisis was a complex and multifaceted conflict with far-reaching consequences. It highlighted the decline of traditional colonial powers, the rise of nationalist movements in the Middle East, and the increasing importance of Cold War dynamics in international relations. For Israel, it temporarily enhanced its military and strategic position, but it also laid the groundwork for future conflicts in the region.

CHAPTER 4: THE SIX-DAY WAR AND ITS AFTERMATH

Prelude to the 1967 War

The Prelude to the 1967 War, also known as the Six-Day War, involves a complex interplay of geopolitical, military, and regional factors that escalated tensions in the Middle East. This period set the stage for one of the most significant conflicts in the history of the Israel-Arab relations, profoundly shaping the region's future.

Regional Tensions:

1. **Arab Nationalism**: The rise of Arab nationalism, particularly under Egyptian President Gamal Abdel Nasser, posed a significant challenge to Israel's existence. Nasser's rhetoric and actions were geared towards uniting the Arab world against Israel.

2. **Palestinian Fedayeen Raids**: Cross-border attacks by Palestinian guerrilla groups, known as Fedayeen, into Israeli territory, largely from Jordan and the Gaza Strip, increased tensions. Israel frequently retaliated with military strikes.

International Context:

1. **Cold War Dynamics**: The Cold War rivalry between the United States and the Soviet Union played a significant role, with the USSR supporting Arab states and the USA inclined towards Israel.

2. **Arms Race**: An arms race in the region was evident, with the Soviet Union supplying weapons to Egypt and Syria, while the United States and Western Europe were key arms suppliers to Israel.

Key Incidents and Developments:

1. **Syrian Border Clashes**: Israel and Syria engaged in repeated skirmishes over the demilitarized zones and the waters of the Jordan River, which were crucial for Israel's agricultural sector.

2. **Egyptian Military Buildup**: In 1967, Nasser began a significant military buildup in the Sinai Peninsula, alarming Israel. The Egyptian army's deployment along Israel's border was perceived as an imminent threat.

Diplomatic Strains:

1. **Blockade of the Straits of Tiran**: In May 1967, Egypt imposed a naval blockade of the Straits of Tiran, a critical maritime passage for Israeli shipping, especially for the port of Eilat. This act was a casus belli for Israel, as it directly threatened its economic lifeline.

2. **Expulsion of UN Peacekeepers**: Egypt demanded the withdrawal of the United Nations Emergency Force (UNEF) from the Sinai Peninsula, which had been stationed there since the 1956 Suez Crisis to act as a buffer between Egyptian and Israeli forces.

3. **Arab League Summit**: Arab leaders held summits where they discussed plans and rhetoric was increasingly hostile towards Israel. The summit contributed to the warlike atmosphere.

Israeli Concerns and Mobilization:

1. **Existential Threat**: The combination of Arab military buildup, hostile rhetoric, and the blockade heightened Israel's perception of an existential threat.

2. **Mobilization of Reserves**: Israel, facing the threat of a multi-front attack, mobilized its

reserves, which put a strain on its economy and increased the urgency for a swift action.

US and Soviet Roles:

1. **Diplomatic Efforts**: Both superpowers made diplomatic efforts to de-escalate tensions but were limited by their respective alliances and the rapidly evolving situation on the ground.

2. **Intelligence and Warnings**: The US and the USSR provided their allies with intelligence and strategic advice, but also contributed to the tensions through their military support.

Media and Public Opinion:

1. **Media War**: The period leading up to the war was marked by a media war, with Arab and Israeli media escalating the situation with their coverage and propaganda.

2. **Public Sentiment**: Public opinion in the Arab world and Israel was increasingly inflamed, creating pressure on governments to act.

The Prelude to the 1967 War was marked by a build-up of military forces, aggressive political rhetoric, and a series of incidents and diplomatic failures that led to the eruption of the Six-Day War. This period was a crucial phase in the long-standing Arab-Israeli conflict, setting the stage for a war that would dramatically alter the geopolitical landscape of the Middle East.

The War and its Immediate Effects

The 1967 Six-Day War, a pivotal conflict in the Middle East, had profound and lasting effects on the region. The war, fought between Israel and the neighboring states of Egypt, Jordan, and Syria, led to a swift and decisive victory for Israel. This conflict not only reshaped the geopolitical landscape of the Middle East but also had far-reaching implications for the Israeli-Arab relations.

The War:

1. **Swift Israeli Offensive**: The war began on June 5, 1967, with a preemptive Israeli air strike that decimated the Egyptian air force. This move was followed by rapid ground offensives.

2. **Multiple Fronts**: Israel simultaneously fought against Egyptian forces in the Sinai Peninsula, Jordanian forces in the West Bank, and Syrian forces in the Golan Heights.

3. **Decisive Victories**: Within six days, Israel achieved a stunning victory, capturing the Sinai Peninsula, the West Bank, East Jerusalem, and the Golan Heights.

Immediate Effects:

1. **Territorial Gains**: Israel's territorial expansion was the most immediate effect of the war. The Sinai Peninsula, Golan Heights, East Jerusalem, and the West Bank were all occupied by Israel, dramatically altering the map of the region.

2. **Jerusalem's Unification**: The capture of East Jerusalem and its subsequent unification with West Jerusalem was a momentous event for Israel, bringing the entire city under its control.

3. **Palestinian Displacement**: The war led to a significant displacement of Palestinians, especially from the West Bank and East Jerusalem, adding to the refugee problem created in 1948.

4. **Military and Political Emboldenment**: Israel's swift victory bolstered its military

reputation and significantly influenced its political stance in the region, fostering a sense of security and strength.

5. **Arab World's Reaction**: The Arab states suffered a severe psychological and military defeat. The loss was a significant blow to Arab nationalism, particularly to Egyptian President Gamal Abdel Nasser's leadership.

6. **Superpower Involvement**: The war heightened the involvement of the US and the USSR in the region. The US emerged as a principal supporter of Israel, while the Soviet Union backed the Arab states.

7. **Reshaping of Alliances**: Post-war, there was a realignment of alliances in the Middle East. Countries reassessed their foreign policies and relationships in light of the new geopolitical reality.

8. **Increased Tensions and Future Conflicts**: The war sowed the seeds for future conflicts, including the War of Attrition and the Yom Kippur War. It entrenched the hostility and mistrust between Israel and its Arab neighbors.

9. **International Diplomacy**: The United Nations' involvement increased, leading to resolutions such as UN Security Council Resolution 242, which called for Israeli withdrawal from occupied territories and the acknowledgment of all states' right to exist.

10. **Jewish Settlements**: The occupation of the West Bank and Gaza Strip led to the establishment of Jewish settlements in these areas, which became a contentious issue in the Israeli-Palestinian conflict.

In summary, the 1967 Six-Day War was a turning point in Middle Eastern history. Its immediate effects, particularly Israel's territorial expansion and the displacement of Palestinians, set the stage for decades of ongoing conflict and negotiations. The war's aftermath reshaped the region's politics, diplomacy, and the very fabric of Israeli and Arab societal and national identities.

Occupation and Settlements in the Captured Territories

The aftermath of the 1967 Six-Day War, specifically the occupation and establishment of settlements in the captured territories, marked a significant and contentious chapter in the history of the Israeli-Palestinian conflict.

Occupation of Territories:

1. **Extensive Control**: Following the war, Israel found itself in control of large territories: the

Sinai Peninsula from Egypt, the Golan Heights from Syria, and the West Bank, including East Jerusalem, from Jordan.

2. **Military Administration**: In the occupied territories, Israel established military administrations to govern the areas. This included enforcing Israeli laws, jurisdiction, and administration.

3. **East Jerusalem Annexation**: Israel's annexation of East Jerusalem was a significant move, declaring the entire city as its capital. This act was met with international criticism and was not widely recognized by the international community.

4. **Status of Territories**: The status of these territories, especially the West Bank and Golan Heights, became central in subsequent peace negotiations and international discussions. The

Sinai Peninsula was later returned to Egypt as part of the 1979 Egypt-Israel Peace Treaty.

Settlements in Captured Territories:

1. **Establishment of Settlements**: Post-1967, Israel began establishing settlements in the occupied territories, including the West Bank, East Jerusalem, and the Golan Heights. These settlements ranged from small outposts to large residential communities.

2. **Political and Ideological Motivations**: The settlements were driven by a mix of security concerns, religious and historical beliefs (especially in areas of biblical significance like Hebron), and political motivations to establish a Jewish presence in these regions.

3. **International View**: The international community, including the United Nations, generally views these settlements as illegal

under international law, particularly the Fourth Geneva Convention, which prohibits an occupying power from transferring its population into the territories it occupies.

4. **Palestinian View and Impact**: For Palestinians, the settlements are seen as an illegal encroachment on land they view as part of a future independent state. This has been a major source of tension and conflict.

5. **Expansion and Growth**: Over the years, the settlement population has grown significantly, further complicating the Israeli-Palestinian conflict. The expansion of settlements has often led to displacement of Palestinian communities and a source of frequent violence and confrontations.

6. **Impact on Peace Process**: The settlements have been a significant stumbling block in peace

negotiations, with Palestinians viewing them as a major obstacle to the creation of a viable Palestinian state.

7. **Security Barrier**: In response to security concerns, Israel began constructing a barrier in the West Bank in the early 2000s, which further heightened tensions. While Israel argues the barrier is necessary for security, Palestinians see it as a tool for annexing territory and controlling their movement.

The occupation and settlements in the territories captured during the 1967 war have deeply affected the dynamics of the Israeli-Palestinian conflict. These developments have not only altered the physical landscape but have also had profound implications for the lives of both Israelis and Palestinians, fueling ongoing conflict, impacting the peace process, and shaping the political discourse within and outside the region.

CHAPTER 5: THE YOM KIPPUR WAR AND PEACE EFFORTS

The 1973 War Explained

The 1973 War, commonly known as the Yom Kippur War, was a pivotal and traumatic conflict in the Middle East, particularly for Israel and the Arab nations, primarily Egypt and Syria. As a seasoned war reporter, I've witnessed the long-lasting impacts of this war on the region's geopolitics and psychology.

Background:

- After the Six-Day War in 1967, where Israel captured significant territories, including the Sinai Peninsula and the Golan Heights, tensions remained high. Egypt and Syria sought to reclaim their lost territories and restore national pride.

- The peace efforts were stagnant, and Arab nations felt a growing frustration over the status quo.

Outbreak of War:

- The war began on October 6, 1973, coinciding with Yom Kippur, the holiest day in the Jewish calendar, and during Ramadan for Muslims. Egypt and Syria launched a surprise attack against Israel.

- The choice of Yom Kippur was strategic, aiming to catch the Israeli Defense Forces at a lower level of readiness.

Egyptian and Syrian Attacks:

- Egypt, led by President Anwar Sadat, crossed the Suez Canal and breached the seemingly impenetrable Bar Lev Line, establishing a stronghold on the eastern bank.

- Syria attacked the Golan Heights, initially making significant advances against the Israeli forces.

Initial Israeli Setbacks and Mobilization:

- Israel, under Prime Minister Golda Meir, was initially caught off guard. The initial days of the war saw Israeli defenses under severe strain.

- However, Israel rapidly mobilized its reserves and counterattacked. Despite heavy losses, Israeli resilience and tactical ingenuity gradually turned the tide.

Turning Points:

- On the Golan front, Israel managed to push back the Syrian forces. The battles were intense and often close-quarter.

- In the Sinai, the Israeli army executed a daring crossing of the Suez Canal, encircling the

Egyptian Third Army and cutting off its supplies.

Superpower Involvement:

- The war saw significant involvement from the superpowers, the USA and the Soviet Union, each backing their respective allies with arms and diplomatic support.

- This superpower brinkmanship brought the Cold War to the Middle East, adding a layer of international tension to the conflict.

Ceasefire and Aftermath:

- A UN-brokered ceasefire was eventually put in place. The war resulted in heavy casualties on both sides and left a psychological scar, particularly in Israel, where the myth of invincibility was shattered.

- Politically, the war set the stage for future peace negotiations. It led to Sadat's historic visit to Jerusalem in 1977 and the subsequent Camp David Accords, which returned Sinai to Egypt and opened a path to peace between Israel and Egypt.

Legacy:

- The Yom Kippur War marked a shift in Arab-Israeli relations. It showed that while military might could not resolve the conflict, diplomacy might.

- The war also led to changes within Israeli society and its military, prompting introspection and reform.

The 1973 War was a complex conflict that reshaped the Middle East. It demonstrated the limits of military solutions in the region's entrenched conflicts and underscored the need for diplomatic efforts, which, though arduous, offered a more sustainable path toward peace and stability in this tumultuous region.

Camp David Accords

The Camp David Accords, a landmark in Middle Eastern history, were a series of agreements between Israel and Egypt, brokered by the United States in 1978. As a war reporter with decades of experience in the region, I've seen firsthand the profound impact these accords had on the trajectory of the Israeli-Arab conflict.

Context and Background:

- Following the 1973 Yom Kippur War, there was a renewed push for peace in the Middle East. The conflict had drained both Israel and Egypt, making the prospect of continued warfare increasingly unpalatable.

- U.S. President Jimmy Carter saw an opportunity to broker peace and invited Egyptian President Anwar Sadat and Israeli Prime Minister Menachem Begin to Camp David, a presidential retreat in Maryland, USA.

Historic Summit at Camp David:

- The summit took place in September 1978. The negotiations were intense, often teetering on the brink of collapse.

- Carter played a pivotal role, shuttling between the two leaders, who rarely met face-to-face, working tirelessly to find common ground.

Key Provisions:

- **Framework for Peace in the Middle East:** This part of the accords laid the groundwork for

Palestinian self-governance in the West Bank and Gaza Strip and aimed to resolve the Palestinian issue in all its aspects.

- **Framework for the Conclusion of a Peace Treaty between Egypt and Israel**: It outlined the steps towards a peace treaty, including the withdrawal of Israeli forces from Sinai, the normalization of relations between the two countries, and the recognition of each other's sovereignty.

Signing of the Peace Treaty:

- In March 1979, following the Camp David Accords, Egypt and Israel signed a formal peace treaty.

- Israel agreed to withdraw from the Sinai Peninsula, which it had occupied since the Six-Day War in 1967.

- In return, Egypt recognized Israel's right to exist and established diplomatic relations, becoming the first Arab country to do so.

Impact and Significance:

- The Camp David Accords were a groundbreaking achievement, marking the first peace agreement between Israel and an Arab state.

- For Egypt, it meant regaining Sinai and setting a precedent for Arab engagement with Israel.

- For Israel, it was a major step towards legitimacy and security in a region where it had previously only known hostility from its neighbors.

Aftermath and Reception:

- In the Arab world, the accords were met with mixed reactions. Many Arab states felt betrayed by Egypt's unilateral move to recognize Israel.

- Sadat was ostracized by the Arab League, and Egypt was suspended from the organization until 1989.

- Tragically, Sadat's peacemaking efforts led to his assassination in 1981 by extremists within Egypt who opposed his policies.

Legacy:

- The Camp David Accords remain a high watermark in Middle East peacemaking. They demonstrated that dialogue and compromise could achieve what years of conflict had not.

- The accords also set a template for future peace efforts, including the 1993 Oslo Accords between Israel and the Palestinians.

The Camp David Accords were a bold step towards peace in a region scarred by decades of conflict. They showed the world that even the most intractable of disputes could find a path to resolution through dialogue and diplomacy. Despite the challenges and setbacks that followed, the accords continue to be a symbol of hope for peace in the Middle East.

The Egypt-Israel Peace Treaty

The Egypt-Israel Peace Treaty, signed on March 26, 1979, marked a pivotal moment in Middle Eastern history and a major milestone in diplomatic efforts to resolve the Arab-Israeli conflict. As a war reporter who's witnessed the repercussions of this historic event, I can attest to its profound significance and enduring impact.

Background:

- The treaty stemmed from the Camp David Accords, facilitated by U.S. President Jimmy Carter, involving Egyptian President Anwar Sadat and Israeli Prime Minister Menachem Begin.

- These negotiations were a continuation of Sadat's groundbreaking 1977 visit to Jerusalem, where he addressed the Knesset (Israeli Parliament), extending a hand of peace.

Key Provisions of the Treaty:

1. **Mutual Recognition**: Egypt became the first Arab country to officially recognize the State of Israel.

2. **Israeli Withdrawal from Sinai**: Israel agreed to withdraw all military and civilian presence from the Sinai Peninsula, which it had occupied since the 1967 Six-Day War.

3. **Demilitarization of Sinai**: The treaty established zones in Sinai where Egyptian and Israeli military forces were limited.

4. **Free Passage Through Waterways**: It guaranteed free passage for Israeli ships through the Suez Canal and recognized the Strait of Tiran and the Gulf of Aqaba as international waterways.

5. **Normalization of Relations**: The two nations agreed to establish normal diplomatic and economic relations, including trade, cultural exchanges, and tourism.

Signing and International Reaction:

- The signing ceremony took place in Washington, D.C., with President Carter playing a key role in finalizing the agreement.

- The international community, particularly the United States, lauded the treaty as a groundbreaking step towards peace in the Middle East.

Impact on Egypt and Israel:

- For Israel, the treaty marked a significant step towards acceptance and security in a region where it was previously surrounded by hostile neighbors.

- For Egypt, regaining the Sinai Peninsula was a matter of national pride and sovereignty.

Reception in the Arab World:

- The treaty was met with severe criticism from many Arab states. Egypt was suspended from the Arab League, and Sadat was viewed as a traitor by some for making peace with Israel.

- The treaty reshaped the geopolitical landscape of the Middle East, leading to a realignment of regional alliances.

Assassination of Anwar Sadat:

- In 1981, Sadat was assassinated by extremists within Egypt, partly in response to his peace agreement with Israel.

- His death highlighted the deep divisions and the high stakes involved in the peace process.

Legacy:

- The Egypt-Israel Peace Treaty remains one of the most significant diplomatic achievements in the Middle East.

- It set a precedent for Arab-Israeli negotiations and paved the way for future peace agreements, like the Oslo Accords between Israel and the Palestinians.

Contemporary Relevance:

- Despite regional upheavals and changes in leadership, the treaty has endured, underscoring a mutual understanding of the benefits of peace over the perils of continued conflict.

- It serves as a reminder that even the most entrenched conflicts can find resolution through sustained diplomatic efforts.

In summary, the Egypt-Israel Peace Treaty was a watershed event that not only altered the course of Egyptian-Israeli relations but also had far-reaching implications for the entire Middle East. Its endurance over decades stands as a testament to the possibility of peace through negotiation, even amidst a landscape often dominated by conflict.

CHAPTER 6: THE FIRST INTIFADA AND OSLO ACCORDS

Rise of the Palestinian Liberation Organization (PLO)

The rise of the Palestinian Liberation Organization (PLO) marks a significant chapter in the Israel-Palestine conflict, one that I've seen evolve dramatically over my years as a war correspondent. Established in 1964, the PLO emerged as a pivotal player, embodying the aspirations and struggles of the Palestinian people.

Formation and Early Years:

- The PLO was formed under the Arab League's auspices, initially perceived as a tool of Arab states to manage the Palestinian issue.

- Ahmed Shukeiri, its first leader, played a crucial role in its early development.

- Initially, the PLO's activities were more political and diplomatic, aiming to gain international recognition for the Palestinian cause.

Shift to Armed Struggle:

- In the late 1960s, under Yasser Arafat's leadership and his faction Fatah, the PLO increasingly adopted armed struggle as a means to achieve Palestinian national goals.

- This period saw numerous guerilla attacks and raids against Israeli targets, both within Israel and across its borders.

International Recognition and Diplomatic Efforts:

- Over the years, the PLO gained significant political recognition. By the mid-1970s, it was seen as the "sole legitimate representative of the

Palestinian people" by over 100 states and gained observer status at the United Nations.

- This diplomatic recognition was a significant achievement, elevating the Palestinian issue on the international stage.

Internal Divisions and Challenges:

- The PLO was not without its internal divisions. Various factions within the organization often had differing ideologies and strategies.

- These divisions were further exacerbated by external pressures, particularly from host countries like Jordan and Lebanon, leading to violent confrontations.

The Lebanon War and Exile:

- The Israeli invasion of Lebanon in 1982, aimed at rooting out the PLO, was a turning point.

- The siege of Beirut and subsequent evacuation of PLO fighters marked a significant setback, forcing the organization to relocate its base to Tunisia.

Shift Towards a Political Solution:

- In the late 1980s, under Arafat's leadership, the PLO began shifting towards a more political approach, recognizing Israel's right to exist and renouncing terrorism.

- This shift paved the way for the Oslo Accords in the 1990s, a significant attempt at peace negotiations between Israel and the Palestinians.

Oslo Accords and the Palestinian Authority:

- The Oslo Accords led to the creation of the Palestinian Authority (PA), seen as a precursor to an independent Palestinian state.

- Arafat's return to Gaza and the West Bank as the head of the PA marked a new phase in Palestinian self-governance, although full statehood remained elusive.

Contemporary Role:

- Today, the PLO remains a central entity in Palestinian politics, though its influence has waned with the rise of other groups like Hamas.

- The organization continues to face challenges, including internal rifts, the struggle for Palestinian unity, and the ongoing conflict with Israel.

The PLO's journey from a liberation movement to a recognized political entity reflects the complexities and evolving dynamics of the Israel-Palestine conflict. As a witness to these changes, it's clear that the PLO has been both a symbol of Palestinian national identity and a participant in the quest for a lasting solution to the conflict.

The First Intifada (1987-1993)

The First Intifada, a pivotal event in the Israel-Palestine conflict, began in December 1987 and lasted until the Oslo Accords in 1993. As a war correspondent, I witnessed this uprising unfold, marked by a shift in the Palestinian resistance tactics and a profound impact on both Palestinian society and Israeli politics.

Origins and Causes:

- The Intifada (Arabic for "shaking off") was largely a spontaneous uprising against the Israeli occupation in the Gaza Strip and the West Bank.

- Years of political frustration, economic hardships, and the absence of a viable political solution fueled the Palestinians' desire for self-determination.

Characteristics of the Intifada:

- Unlike previous conflicts, the First Intifada was characterized by widespread participation of Palestinian civilians, including women and children.

- Protesters primarily used stones, Molotov cocktails, and erected barricades, symbolizing a David vs. Goliath struggle against a well-equipped military.

- Civil disobedience, including strikes and boycotts of Israeli products, was a significant aspect of the Intifada.

Israeli Response:

- The Israeli military response was harsh, aiming to quell the uprising through curfews, arrests, and a policy infamously termed as "breaking the bones" strategy.

- The conflict resulted in a high casualty rate, with thousands of Palestinians killed or injured, and many more arrested.

Impact on Palestinian Society:

- The Intifada saw the emergence of local leadership within Palestinian territories, reducing the influence of external Palestinian groups.

- Grassroots organizations, often linked with factions like Fatah, Hamas, and the Islamic Jihad, gained prominence.

- The uprising also saw the rise of Hamas, which challenged the PLO's dominance.

Political Ramifications:

- The Intifada significantly impacted Israeli politics, leading to a split in public opinion and mounting international pressure for a peaceful resolution.

- It exposed the unsustainable nature of the occupation and highlighted the need for a political solution to the Israeli-Palestinian conflict.

Path to Oslo Accords:

- The prolonged nature of the uprising and the international attention it garnered eventually led to secret negotiations between the PLO and Israel.

- These talks culminated in the Oslo Accords of 1993, which marked a significant though controversial step towards a two-state solution.

Legacy:

- The First Intifada is remembered for its grassroots nature, widespread participation, and its role in bringing the Palestinian issue back to the forefront of international politics.

- It highlighted the complexities of the Israeli-Palestinian conflict and set the stage for future negotiations and subsequent uprisings.

As I reflect on those years, the images of young Palestinians facing tanks with stones in hand and the cries for independence echo the sentiments of a population yearning for statehood and an end to the occupation. The First Intifada reshaped the political landscape of the region and remains a significant chapter in the history of the Israel-Palestine conflict.

The Oslo Accords and their Impact

The Oslo Accords, a series of agreements between Israel and the Palestine Liberation Organization (PLO), marked a significant turn in the Israel-Palestine conflict. As a war reporter who has observed this region's tensions for decades, the Oslo Accords stood out as a rare moment of hope amidst a history marred by violence and distrust.

Signing of the Oslo Accords:

- The Accords, named after the Norwegian city where the initial secret negotiations took place, were signed in 1993 and 1995.

- The iconic image of Israeli Prime Minister Yitzhak Rabin shaking hands with PLO leader Yasser Arafat, with U.S. President Bill Clinton standing between them, symbolized a potential new era of peace.

Key Provisions:

- The Oslo I Accord, signed in 1993, established the Palestinian Authority (PA), granting limited self-governance in parts of the West Bank and Gaza Strip.

- Oslo II, signed in 1995, divided the West Bank into Areas A, B, and C, with varying degrees of Palestinian and Israeli control and responsibility.

Impact and Challenges:

- The Accords were a significant breakthrough, being the first direct agreement between the two parties and recognizing each other's legitimacy.

- They initiated a peace process with the aim of resolving core issues like borders, settlements, security, and the status of Jerusalem in a final status agreement.

Controversies and Opposition:

- Many Palestinians felt the Accords did not sufficiently address key issues such as Israeli settlements, borders, the right of return for Palestinian refugees, and the status of Jerusalem.

- In Israel, the Accords faced opposition from those who felt they compromised Israel's security and territorial integrity.

Assassination of Yitzhak Rabin:

- The peace process faced a significant setback with the assassination of Prime Minister Rabin in 1995 by a right-wing Israeli extremist, an event that profoundly shocked and saddened me.

- Rabin's death was a stark reminder of the deep divisions within Israeli society regarding the peace process.

Subsequent Developments:

- The peace process, post-Oslo, faced numerous challenges, including continued settlement activity, outbreaks of violence, and political changes in leadership.

- The failure to address final status issues and mutual accusations of non-compliance led to a gradual erosion of trust between the parties.

Legacy of the Oslo Accords:

- The Oslo Accords, despite their limitations and the failure to achieve lasting peace, represented a significant step toward recognizing the mutual legitimacy and national aspirations of both Israelis and Palestinians.

- They laid the groundwork for future negotiations, even as they highlighted the complexities and deep-seated issues within the conflict.

As a journalist who has witnessed the ebb and flow of this conflict, the Oslo Accords stand out as a moment where peace seemed within grasp, despite the challenges and heartbreaks that followed. Their legacy continues to influence the contours of the Israel-Palestine discourse, serving both as a symbol of hope and a reminder of the hurdles yet to be overcome in the pursuit of a lasting resolution.

CHAPTER 7: THE SECOND INTIFADA AND CONTINUED CONFLICT

Causes and Course of the Second Intifada

The Second Intifada, also known as the Al-Aqsa Intifada, was a period of intensified Israeli-Palestinian violence that began in late September 2000 and lasted until around 2005. This conflict marked a significant and tragic chapter in the history of the region, characterized by a level of violence and bitterness that overshadowed the hopes raised by the Oslo Accords. As a war reporter, I witnessed firsthand the transformation of the conflict's nature during this period.

Causes of the Second Intifada:

1. **Collapse of the Peace Process**: The failure of the Camp David Summit in July 2000, where

Israeli Prime Minister Ehud Barak and Palestinian Authority President Yasser Arafat couldn't reach a final agreement, significantly contributed to the tensions. Key issues like the status of Jerusalem remained unresolved.

2. **Ariel Sharon's Visit to the Temple Mount**: The immediate catalyst for the Intifada was the visit of Ariel Sharon, then the leader of the Israeli opposition, to the Temple Mount/Haram al-Sharif in Jerusalem. Palestinians viewed this as a provocative act, as the site holds religious and national significance to both Jews and Muslims.

3. **Long-Standing Grievances**: Palestinians were frustrated by the ongoing occupation, settlement expansion, and the perceived failure of the peace process to improve their living conditions.

Course of the Second Intifada:

1. **Initial Outbreak**: The Intifada began with widespread protests and riots by Palestinians, which escalated into armed confrontations.

2. **Israeli Response**: The Israeli military response was robust, involving air strikes, tank incursions, and targeted assassinations of suspected militants.

3. **Suicide Bombings and Attacks**: The Intifada saw a significant increase in suicide bombings and attacks by Palestinian militants against Israeli civilians and soldiers.

4. **Operation Defensive Shield**: In 2002, Israel launched a large-scale military operation in the West Bank, aimed at dismantling the infrastructure of terrorist groups. This operation led to significant casualties and destruction.

Impact of the Second Intifada:

1. **High Casualties**: The violence resulted in a high number of casualties on both sides, with a significant civilian toll.

2. **Hardening of Attitudes**: The Intifada led to a hardening of attitudes among Israelis and Palestinians, reducing the prospects for a negotiated peace.

3. **Security Measures**: Israel increased its security measures, including the construction of the West Bank barrier, which it claimed was necessary to prevent attacks. Palestinians saw this as a land grab and a tool for further occupation.

4. **Political Changes**: The conflict led to significant political changes in Israeli and Palestinian societies, with a shift towards more hardline leadership on both sides.

End of the Intifada:

- The intensity of the conflict gradually decreased by 2005, partly due to Israeli military operations, the death of Yasser Arafat in 2004, and changes in Palestinian leadership.

- The Second Intifada left a legacy of mistrust and trauma, significantly impacting the regional political landscape and the lives of ordinary Israelis and Palestinians.

As someone who reported from the ground during this turbulent time, the Second Intifada was a stark reminder of the deep-seated animosities and complexities of the Israeli-Palestinian conflict. It underscored the urgent need for a durable and just solution, yet simultaneously illuminated the daunting challenges that such a pursuit entails.

The Separation Barrier and International Response

The construction of the Separation Barrier by Israel, often referred to as the "West Bank barrier" or "apartheid wall" by Palestinians, marked a significant and contentious development in the Israeli-Palestinian conflict. As a war reporter, I observed the profound impact this structure had on the ground, altering the landscape and lives of countless individuals in the region.

The Separation Barrier:

1. **Construction and Purpose**: Israel began constructing the barrier in 2002, during the Second Intifada, with the stated aim of preventing terrorist attacks. The barrier consists of fences, vehicle-barrier trenches, electronic fences, and concrete walls.

2. **Route of the Barrier**: The barrier's route, snaking through the West Bank, often deviates from the Green Line (the 1949 Armistice Line) and encroaches on Palestinian land. This has led to the isolation of Palestinian communities and the effective annexation of parts of the West Bank.

Impact on Palestinians:

1. **Restriction of Movement**: The barrier significantly restricts the movement of Palestinians, affecting their access to farmland, jobs, healthcare, and education.

2. **Economic and Social Impact**: Many Palestinian villages and towns were divided, impacting local economies and separating families.

3. **Land Confiscation**: The construction often involved the confiscation of Palestinian land, contributing to further tensions.

International Response:

1. **International Court of Justice (ICJ) Opinion**: In 2004, the ICJ issued an advisory opinion, declaring the barrier illegal where it deviates into occupied Palestinian territory. It called for the barrier to be dismantled and for affected Palestinians to be compensated.

2. **UN General Assembly**: Following the ICJ opinion, the UN General Assembly demanded that Israel comply with the ICJ's ruling. However, Israel continued the construction, citing security concerns.

3. **International Criticism**: Many international entities, including the European Union and human rights organizations, criticized the

barrier. They argued that while Israel has the right to protect its citizens, the route of the barrier and its impact on Palestinians are disproportionate and counterproductive to peace efforts.

4. **Israeli Perspective**: Israel defends the barrier as a necessary security measure that has significantly reduced terrorist attacks. It argues that the barrier is temporary and can be adjusted in future peace negotiations.

Current Status:

- As of my last reports in the region, the barrier remains a highly visible and controversial symbol of the conflict. It continues to be a source of hardship for Palestinians and a point of contention in peace negotiations.

- The barrier's existence and its implications continue to be a topic of international debate, reflecting the broader complexities and challenges of the Israeli-Palestinian conflict.

Reporting from the field, the barrier's imposing presence always struck me as a stark physical manifestation of the deep divisions and enduring conflict between Israelis and Palestinians. It's a reminder of the unresolved political, security, and humanitarian issues that continue to fuel tensions in this storied land.

Shifts in Israeli and Palestinian Leadership

In my years covering the Israeli-Palestinian conflict, I've witnessed several pivotal shifts in leadership on both sides. These changes have often reflected and influenced the evolving dynamics of the conflict.

Shifts in Israeli Leadership:

1. **Diverse Coalition Governments**: Israel has seen a range of coalition governments, often comprising parties with differing ideologies. These coalitions have influenced policy directions regarding the Palestinian issue, oscillating between hardline and more conciliatory approaches.

2. **The Rise of Right-Wing Politics**: Over the years, there's been a noticeable shift towards right-wing politics in Israel, emphasizing security and less inclined towards significant territorial compromises. Leaders like Benjamin Netanyahu have embodied this shift.

3. **Impact of Internal Politics**: Domestic issues, including corruption scandals and public opinion, have significantly impacted the tenure and policies of Israeli leaders, often affecting negotiations and relations with Palestinians.

Shifts in Palestinian Leadership:

1. **From Arafat to Abbas**: The death of Yasser Arafat in 2004 and the subsequent leadership of Mahmoud Abbas marked a significant shift. Abbas has been seen as a more moderate leader, focusing on diplomacy and cooperation with international bodies.

2. **Hamas' Ascendancy in Gaza**: The 2006 Palestinian legislative election saw Hamas winning a surprising majority. This led to internal Palestinian conflicts, culminating in Hamas seizing control of Gaza in 2007, leading to a geographical and political split between the West Bank and Gaza.

3. **Fatah's Struggle and Fragmentation**: Fatah, historically the dominant faction in the PLO, has faced challenges in maintaining unity, dealing with corruption allegations, and

addressing growing dissatisfaction among Palestinians.

Implications of Leadership Changes:

1. **Impact on Peace Process**: Leadership changes have directly impacted the peace process. Israeli leaders' willingness to negotiate and Palestinian leaders' ability to represent and unify different factions have been crucial.

2. **Internal Political Stability**: Both Israeli and Palestinian political landscapes have experienced fragmentation and instability, affecting their ability to engage effectively in peace negotiations.

3. **International Relations**: Changes in leadership have also influenced relationships with key international players, including the United States, the European Union, and Arab countries. These relationships are vital in

shaping the external support and pressure exerted on both parties.

Current Trends:

- As of my last reports, there's a sense of stagnation and skepticism on both sides. New generations of Israelis and Palestinians are growing up amidst ongoing conflict, often with differing views from their predecessors.

- The leadership on both sides faces challenges in addressing the aspirations and frustrations of their people, particularly in the context of a protracted and seemingly intractable conflict.

Through the lens of a seasoned war reporter, these leadership shifts are not just political maneuvers; they represent the hopes, fears, and changing realities of the people living through this enduring conflict. Each change in leadership brings its unique narrative to this complex tapestry, reflecting the deep-rooted and multifaceted nature of the Israeli-Palestinian saga.

CHAPTER 8: THE GAZA STRIP: DISENGAGEMENT AND HAMAS

Israeli Disengagement from Gaza (2005)

As a war reporter with decades of experience, I witnessed firsthand the Israeli Disengagement from Gaza in 2005, a significant and controversial moment in the Israeli-Palestinian conflict. Here's a narrative that captures the essence of those events:

Background of the Plan:

- **Prime Minister Ariel Sharon's Initiative**: In 2003, Israeli Prime Minister Ariel Sharon, once a staunch supporter of settlements, surprised many by announcing a plan for unilateral disengagement from the Gaza Strip. This plan involved evacuating all Israeli settlements in Gaza and four in the West Bank.

- **Strategic Shift**: The disengagement was seen as a strategic shift by Israel. Amidst the ongoing Second Intifada, it was a move to enhance security and reduce friction between Israeli settlers and Palestinians. It also aimed to improve Israel's international standing.

Implementation of the Disengagement:

- **Evacuation of Settlers**: In August 2005, the Israeli military began the evacuation. It was a deeply emotional and turbulent process. Settlers, many of whom had lived in Gaza for generations, were forcibly removed from their homes, leading to scenes of grief and anger.

- **Military Withdrawal**: Following the civilian evacuation, the Israeli military withdrew, marking the end of 38 years of Israeli presence in Gaza. The vacated land was handed over to the Palestinian Authority.

Reactions and Aftermath:

- **Mixed Reactions in Israel:** The disengagement was highly divisive within Israel. While some viewed it as a necessary step towards peace and security, others saw it as a betrayal. The withdrawal sparked intense debate about the future of Israeli settlements and the peace process.

- **Palestinian Response:** Palestinians had mixed reactions. While some saw it as a victory for armed resistance, others were cautious, viewing it as a unilateral move that didn't address broader issues like Palestinian statehood or the status of Jerusalem.

- **Rise of Hamas:** Post-disengagement, Hamas' influence in Gaza grew. In 2006, Hamas won the Palestinian legislative elections and subsequently seized control of Gaza in 2007, leading to a split between the Gaza Strip, governed by Hamas, and the West Bank, under the Palestinian Authority.

Impact on the Conflict:

- **Security Concerns**: The disengagement did not bring the anticipated security. Rocket fire from Gaza into Israel continued, leading to several military confrontations in the ensuing years.

- **Impact on Peace Process**: The unilateral nature of the disengagement left many issues unresolved and was followed by a deterioration in Israeli-Palestinian relations.

- **Internal Israeli Politics**: The disengagement had lasting effects on Israeli politics, reshaping the debate on settlements and influencing the approach of future leaders.

From the ground, the disengagement was a vivid illustration of the complexities and emotions inherent in the Israeli-Palestinian conflict. It was a moment of significant change, yet underscored the enduring challenges in reaching a comprehensive peace agreement. The echoes of those days in 2005 are still felt in the region's ongoing struggle for peace and stability.

The Rise of Hamas and Internal Palestinian Conflict

The rise of Hamas and the internal Palestinian conflict present a critical chapter in the Middle East's complex narrative. As a war correspondent, I have witnessed the intricate dynamics that have shaped this part of the story.

The Emergence of Hamas:

- **Founding**: Hamas, an acronym for "Harakat al-Muqawama al-Islamiya" (Islamic Resistance Movement), was founded in 1987 during the First Intifada. It emerged from the Gaza wing of the Muslim Brotherhood.

- **Charter and Ideology**: Hamas' 1988 charter called for the establishment of an Islamic state in Palestine. It opposed the Oslo Accords, rejecting Israel's right to exist.

Hamas's Growing Influence:

- **Social Services**: Beyond its militant activities, Hamas gained popularity by providing social services in Gaza, often stepping in where the Palestinian Authority (PA) was seen as corrupt or ineffective.

- **Election Victory**: In 2006, Hamas won a surprising victory in the Palestinian legislative elections. This win was attributed to its anti-corruption stance and the failure of the PA to achieve significant progress in peace talks with Israel.

Internal Palestinian Conflict:

- **Fatah-Hamas Split**: The electoral victory led to tensions with Fatah, the leading party in the PA. These tensions soon escalated into violent clashes.

- **Takeover of Gaza**: In 2007, Hamas forcibly took control of the Gaza Strip after intense fighting with Fatah forces. This event split the Palestinian territories into two political entities: the West Bank under the PA and the Gaza Strip under Hamas.

Impact on Israeli-Palestinian Conflict:

- **Isolation of Gaza**: Following the takeover, Israel and Egypt imposed a blockade on Gaza, citing security concerns over Hamas, which is recognized by many countries, including Israel, the United States, and the European Union, as a terrorist organization.

- **Continued Conflict**: Hamas's control of Gaza led to several military confrontations with Israel, marked by rocket fire from Gaza and retaliatory Israeli airstrikes.

International Response and Challenges:

- **Diplomatic Isolation**: Hamas's refusal to recognize Israel, renounce violence, and accept previous Israeli-Palestinian agreements led to its international isolation.

- **Humanitarian Crisis in Gaza**: The blockade and recurring conflicts have resulted in a humanitarian crisis in Gaza, affecting millions of civilians.

- **Attempts at Reconciliation**: Efforts have been made to reconcile Hamas and Fatah, but these have largely been unsuccessful, complicating any potential for a unified Palestinian front in peace talks with Israel.

As someone who has reported from the front lines, I have seen how the rise of Hamas and the ensuing internal Palestinian conflict have not only reshaped Palestinian politics but have also had profound implications for the wider Israeli-Palestinian conflict, complicating the quest for a lasting peace in the region.

Gaza Wars: 2008, 2012, 2014

As a war reporter, I have seen firsthand the devastation and complexities of the Gaza Wars of 2008, 2012, and 2014. Each conflict reflected deep-seated issues and had significant impacts on both Israelis and Palestinians.

Gaza War of 2008-2009 (Operation Cast Lead):

- **Causes**: Tensions escalated due to rocket fire from Gaza into Israeli territory and a blockade imposed by Israel and Egypt. Israel's objective was to stop these rocket attacks and arms smuggling into Gaza.

- **Timeline and Tactics**: The war began in late December 2008, with a massive Israeli air campaign followed by a ground invasion. Israel targeted Hamas military infrastructure but also hit civilian areas.

- **Humanitarian Impact**: The war resulted in significant civilian casualties and destruction in Gaza. International organizations raised concerns about potential war crimes by both sides.

Gaza War of 2012 (Operation Pillar of Defense):

- **Trigger**: An escalation in rocket fire from Gaza and targeted killings by Israel, including the assassination of a top Hamas leader, led to this conflict.

- **Military Operations**: Lasting just over a week, this conflict primarily involved airstrikes and artillery fire. Israel again aimed to stop rocket attacks.

- **Ceasefire**: An Egypt-brokered ceasefire ended the conflict. However, the underlying issues remained unresolved.

Gaza War of 2014 (Operation Protective Edge):

- **Prelude**: The kidnapping and murder of three Israeli teenagers, followed by the retaliatory killing of a Palestinian teen, heightened tensions.

- **Conflict Dynamics**: The war lasted seven weeks, involving an Israeli ground invasion and extensive bombardment. Hamas and other groups fired rockets deep into Israeli territory.

- **Destruction and Loss of Life**: There was substantial loss of life, particularly in Gaza, with thousands of deaths, mostly civilians, and widespread destruction of infrastructure.

- **International Reaction**: The international community expressed alarm at the humanitarian situation in Gaza. There were protests worldwide against Israeli actions and blockades.

Common Themes and Aftermath:

- **Cycles of Violence**: Each conflict followed a pattern of escalation, military engagement, and temporary ceasefires, without addressing the root causes.

- **Humanitarian Crisis in Gaza**: The wars exacerbated the already dire humanitarian situation in Gaza, with significant impacts on health, education, and the economy.

- **International Diplomacy**: These conflicts saw increased efforts at international diplomacy to broker ceasefires, yet a long-term solution remained elusive.

- **Impact on Public Opinion**: Each war affected public opinion regionally and globally, often polarizing views on the Israeli-Palestinian conflict.

Having witnessed these events, it's clear that the Gaza Wars symbolize the enduring and tragic nature of the Israeli-Palestinian conflict, highlighting the urgent need for a sustainable and just resolution to this decades-long struggle.

CHAPTER 9: RECENT DEVELOPMENTS AND ESCALATIONS

Trump's Jerusalem Decision and its Repercussions

Donald Trump's decision in 2017 to recognize Jerusalem as the capital of Israel and move the U.S. Embassy there was one of the most significant and contentious acts of his presidency, particularly in terms of Middle Eastern diplomacy.

The Decision:

- **Announcement**: Trump officially declared the recognition of Jerusalem as Israel's capital in December 2017, breaking with decades of U.S. policy that had refrained from such a move to maintain a neutral stance in the Israeli-Palestinian conflict.

- **Embassy Move**: The U.S. Embassy was relocated from Tel Aviv to Jerusalem in May 2018, coinciding with the 70th anniversary of the founding of the State of Israel.

Repercussions:

- **Palestinian Response**: Palestinians, who claim East Jerusalem as the capital of a future Palestinian state, were outraged. The Palestinian Authority saw this as a blatant disregard for their claims and rights.

- **Violent Clashes and Protests**: The decision sparked widespread protests in the Palestinian territories and across the Muslim world. Clashes between Palestinian protesters and Israeli forces resulted in multiple deaths and injuries.

- **International Reaction**: The move was widely condemned by the international community. Several countries reaffirmed their commitment to a two-state solution, with East Jerusalem as the capital of a future Palestinian state.

- **Impact on Peace Process**: This decision was seen as a significant setback to the Israeli-Palestinian peace process. It fueled skepticism about the U.S.'s role as an unbiased mediator in the conflict.

- **Regional Diplomacy**: Some Arab countries expressed strong opposition, while others were more muted, reflecting a complex regional landscape where alliances and priorities were shifting.

Long-term Implications:

- **Shift in U.S. Policy**: Trump's decision marked a dramatic shift in U.S. foreign policy in the Middle East and was a fulfillment of a campaign promise that appealed to his evangelical Christian base and pro-Israel advocates.

- **Palestinian Authority's Stance**: The Palestinian leadership cut off diplomatic talks with the U.S. administration, questioning America's role as a peace broker.

- **Normalization of Relations**: Despite initial outrage, some Arab countries later normalized relations with Israel as part of the Abraham Accords, indicating a shifting regional dynamic.

As a war reporter, I saw how this decision not only affected high-level diplomatic relations but also the lives of ordinary people. The move heightened tensions and despair among Palestinians and emboldened Israeli hardliners, illustrating the deeply emotional and symbolic significance of Jerusalem in the conflict. The reverberations of this decision continue to be felt in the ongoing struggle for peace and stability in the region.

The Abraham Accords

The Abraham Accords, a series of normalization agreements between Israel and several Arab countries, marked a significant shift in the Middle East diplomatic landscape. These accords, brokered by the United States during the Trump administration, began with agreements between Israel, the United Arab Emirates (UAE), and Bahrain.

Key Elements of the Abraham Accords:

1. **Normalization of Relations**: The accords led to the establishment of formal diplomatic relations between Israel and the UAE, Bahrain, Sudan, and Morocco. This included opening

embassies, initiating direct flights, and promoting trade and tourism.

2. **Economic and Technological Cooperation**: The agreements opened doors for significant economic collaborations, including investments, technological partnerships, and joint ventures in various sectors like tourism, health, energy, and technology.

3. **Security and Strategic Alliances**: The accords facilitated deeper security cooperation against common threats, notably Iran's regional influence and activities. They also aimed to stabilize the region and create a united front against terrorism and extremism.

4. **Cultural and Religious Exchange**: There was an emphasis on cultural and religious exchange to foster mutual understanding,

including facilitating visits to religious sites in Israel for Muslims from these Arab countries.

Implications and Impact:

- **Shift in Arab-Israeli Relations**: Historically, Arab nations had conditioned normalization with Israel on resolving the Palestinian issue. The Abraham Accords broke with this tradition, signaling a new approach in some Arab countries' foreign policies towards Israel.

- **Palestinian Response**: The Palestinians strongly criticized the accords, seeing them as a betrayal of the Arab Peace Initiative and a blow to their aspirations for statehood. They felt sidelined as the focus shifted away from the Israeli-Palestinian conflict.

- **Regional Dynamics**: The accords realigned regional alliances, with shared concerns about

Iran's regional activities being a significant driving force.

- **U.S. Foreign Policy**: The accords were a major foreign policy achievement for the Trump administration, showing a new way of approaching Middle East diplomacy.

- **Continuation under Biden Administration**: The Biden administration has supported and sought to build upon the Abraham Accords, seeing them as a positive development for regional stability.

Personal Reflection as a War Reporter: From my perspective, having witnessed decades of conflict in the region, the Abraham Accords were both a milestone and a source of controversy. While they represented a move towards normalization and peace between Israel and some Arab nations, they also highlighted the complexities and shifting priorities in the region. The

Palestinian issue, once central to Arab-Israeli relations, seemed to take a back seat, raising questions about the future of the Israeli-Palestinian peace process. The accords underscored a changing Middle East, where new alliances were being formed based on shared interests and concerns, particularly regarding Iran.

The 2021 Escalation and Ceasefire

The 2021 Escalation and Ceasefire in the Israel-Palestine conflict was a significant episode of violence, marking one of the most intense periods of conflict between Israel and Palestinian militants, particularly Hamas, since the 2014 Gaza War.

Background and Causes:

1. **Tensions in East Jerusalem**: The immediate trigger was the potential eviction of Palestinian families from the Sheikh Jarrah neighborhood

in East Jerusalem, a move seen by Palestinians and their supporters as part of broader Israeli efforts to change the demographic balance of the city.

2. **Clashes at Al-Aqsa Mosque**: Tensions escalated into clashes between Palestinian worshippers and Israeli police at the Al-Aqsa Mosque compound, a site sacred to both Muslims and Jews, during the holy month of Ramadan.

3. **Gaza Rocket Fire**: In response to the events in East Jerusalem, Hamas and other militant groups in Gaza began firing rockets into Israeli territory.

4. **Israeli Airstrikes**: Israel responded with airstrikes on Gaza, targeting what it said were militant positions, infrastructure, and personnel.

Course of the Conflict:

- **Duration**: The conflict lasted 11 days, from May 10 to May 21, 2021.

- **Rocket Attacks and Airstrikes**: Hundreds of rockets were launched from Gaza towards Israeli cities, leading to civilian casualties and damage. Israel's Iron Dome missile defense system intercepted many of these rockets. In Gaza, Israeli airstrikes caused significant destruction and loss of life, including civilians.

- **International Involvement**: The United States, Egypt, and other international actors engaged in intensive diplomatic efforts to de-escalate the situation.

- **Media Coverage**: The conflict attracted global media attention, with live coverage of rocket attacks and airstrikes. Social media platforms also played a significant role in shaping public opinion and disseminating information.

Ceasefire Agreement:

- **Egyptian Mediation**: Egypt played a key role in mediating between Israel and Hamas, leading to a ceasefire agreement.

- **Terms of the Ceasefire**: The ceasefire, which came into effect on May 21, was unconditional and aimed to halt all hostilities.

- **Aftermath**: Following the ceasefire, there was a period of relative calm, but underlying issues remained unresolved.

Reflection as a War Reporter: As a war reporter with decades of experience, I've seen many cycles of violence in the region, but the 2021 escalation was notably intense and rapid. It highlighted enduring tensions over East Jerusalem and the fragility of peace efforts. The scenes in Gaza were heart-wrenching, with entire families suffering under the bombardment. In Israel, the fear and disruption caused by rocket attacks were palpable. The ceasefire brought relief but also a sobering recognition that without addressing the root causes, such eruptions of violence are likely to recur. The international community's role in brokering peace, particularly Egypt's mediation, was crucial, yet the path to a lasting resolution remains fraught with challenges.

CHAPTER 10: THE 2023 CONFLICT: A TURNING POINT

The October 2023 Conflict

The events of October 2023 stand out as a significant turning point, marked by unprecedented violence and humanitarian crisis.

In the early hours of October 7, 2023, Hamas, along with other Palestinian militant groups, launched a coordinated and massive assault on Israel from the Gaza Strip. Codenamed "Operation Al-Aqsa Flood," this attack was unparalleled in its scale and ferocity. Over 2,200 rockets rained down on Israel in just 20 minutes, overwhelming its Iron Dome missile defense system. Simultaneously, approximately 1,500 militants infiltrated Israeli territory using explosives, bulldozers, and even paragliders, attacking military outposts and civilian areas alike.

The attack left a trail of destruction and despair. Families in their homes and attendees at an outdoor music festival were among the targets, resulting in around 1,200 dead and hundreds taken hostage in just a few hours. The shock and horror of these events were palpable in the streets of Tel Aviv, where survivors, dazed and wounded, recounted the nightmare to rescuers and journalists.

Israel's response was swift and severe. For the first time in half a century, it declared war and implemented a comprehensive siege on the Gaza Strip, cutting off essential supplies like water, electricity, food, and fuel. The ensuing aerial bombardment and ground invasion by the Israeli military were devastating. Gaza, already reeling under years of blockades and previous conflicts, faced a humanitarian catastrophe. Hospitals overflowed, essential supplies ran critically low, and the threat of disease loomed large due to unburied bodies and destroyed infrastructure.

More than 1.4 million Palestinians were displaced internally, with their homes reduced to rubble. The images of destroyed neighborhoods, grieving families, and desperate attempts to salvage the remains of a normal life were heartbreaking. The siege and continuous airstrikes created conditions in Gaza that were worse than any previous conflict, eclipsing the death toll and destruction of the 2008 and 2014 Gaza Wars.

Negotiations for a ceasefire were complex and fraught with challenges. On one side, Israel sought to weaken Hamas's military capabilities and free the hostages. On the other, Hamas demanded the lifting of the siege and the release of Palestinian prisoners. The international community, including the United Nations, called for an immediate ceasefire and condemned the violence, but finding a path to peace seemed elusive.

As of November 2023, the conflict had resulted in a significant shift in the regional geopolitical landscape. The unity among Palestinian factions was tested, and the international community's response reflected growing concerns about the long-term implications of the conflict. For those of us who have covered this conflict for years, the October 2023 events are a stark reminder of the fragile and volatile nature of the Israel-Palestine situation, underscoring the urgent need for a sustainable and just resolution to this decades-long conflict.

The Course of the Conflict

The October 2023 conflict between Israel and Palestinian militant groups, notably Hamas, marked a significant escalation in the long-standing Israel-Palestine conflict. As a war correspondent with decades of experience in the region, I witnessed first-hand the unfolding of this devastating chapter.

Early Assault and Israeli Response The conflict was initiated by a well-coordinated and unprecedented offensive from Hamas, dubbed "Operation Al-Aqsa Flood". In the early hours of October 7, over 2,200 rockets were launched towards Israel, creating widespread panic and chaos. These attacks were accompanied by ground incursions by militants, targeting both military and civilian areas in Israel. The immediate impact was staggering: approximately 1,200 Israelis were killed within hours, and numerous others were taken hostage.

Israel's response was swift and severe. For the first time in 50 years, the nation declared war, initiating a comprehensive siege on the Gaza Strip. This response included a massive aerial bombardment campaign aimed at Hamas and other militant targets. However, the impacts of this campaign were far-reaching, devastating large parts of the Gaza Strip and exacerbating the already dire humanitarian situation.

Humanitarian Crisis in Gaza The Israeli siege led to critical shortages of essential supplies in Gaza, including food, water, and medical supplies. Hospitals, overwhelmed by the influx of casualties, struggled to cope with the limited resources available. The airstrikes led to massive internal displacement, with over 1.4 million Palestinians forced to flee their homes.

International Response and Efforts for Ceasefire The international community reacted with alarm to the escalating violence. The United Nations, along with various nations, called for an immediate ceasefire and condemned the severe humanitarian impact of the conflict. Despite these calls, reaching a ceasefire proved challenging due to the complex demands from both sides. Hamas sought the lifting of the Israeli siege and the release of Palestinian prisoners, while Israel focused on weakening Hamas's military capabilities and securing the release of hostages.

Negotiations and Continuing Tensions As negotiations for a ceasefire continued, the region remained tense. The extensive destruction in Gaza and the high casualty toll left deep scars, both physically and psychologically, on the Palestinian population. The conflict also had broader geopolitical implications, affecting regional dynamics and international relations.

Throughout this period, the stories of human suffering and resilience were heart-wrenching. Families torn apart by loss, children traumatized by the sounds of war, and the unwavering spirit of people amid ruins painted a picture of the harsh realities of this conflict.

As the situation continued to evolve, the need for a sustainable and just resolution to the Israel-Palestine conflict became more apparent. The October 2023 conflict, with its unprecedented scale and impact, served as a somber reminder of the urgent need for peace in a region long plagued by violence and turmoil.

International and Regional Responses

The October 2023 conflict between Israel and Palestinian factions, primarily Hamas, prompted a wide array of international and regional responses. As a seasoned war correspondent, I observed these reactions unfold in real-time, reflecting the complexities and geopolitical sensitivities of the Israel-Palestine issue.

United Nations and Global Diplomacy The United Nations was quick to respond, with the General

Assembly and the Security Council holding emergency sessions. Calls for an immediate ceasefire were strong, emphasizing the dire humanitarian situation in Gaza. Despite these efforts, reaching a consensus among key players proved challenging due to differing views on the conflict's root causes and solutions.

United States' Stance The United States, a key ally of Israel, faced a diplomatic tightrope. While supporting Israel's right to self-defense, there was also significant pressure, both domestically and internationally, to address the humanitarian crisis in Gaza and push for a ceasefire. U.S. efforts focused on back-channel negotiations, attempting to balance its strategic alliance with Israel and the need for stability in the region.

European Union and Individual European Countries European nations expressed concern over the escalation and the humanitarian impact. The

European Union called for restraint and a ceasefire. Individual countries like Germany, France, and the UK echoed these sentiments, highlighting the need for a peaceful resolution. However, their influence on the ground was limited.

Middle Eastern Responses The conflict had a significant impact on the Middle East. Egypt and Jordan, historically mediators in the Israeli-Palestinian conflict, worked towards facilitating talks for a ceasefire. Their unique position as Arab nations with diplomatic ties to Israel placed them at the forefront of these efforts.

Other regional players, including Saudi Arabia and the United Arab Emirates, who had recently normalized relations with Israel, found themselves balancing their new diplomatic ties with public sympathy for the Palestinians. Iran, a long-time supporter of Hamas, condemned Israel's actions and called for regional unity against what they termed as aggression.

Humanitarian Organizations and NGOs International humanitarian organizations, including the Red Cross and Médecins Sans Frontières, were actively involved in providing medical aid and support to civilians in Gaza. The UN agencies, particularly UNRWA, were instrumental in coordinating international aid efforts, despite facing challenges due to the blockade and the destruction of infrastructure.

Public Opinion and Protests Globally, the conflict reignited public interest in the Israel-Palestine issue. Protests and demonstrations in various cities across the world, including in Europe, the Middle East, and the United States, showcased the global divide in opinions and the emotive nature of the conflict.

In summary, the international and regional responses to the October 2023 conflict were a mosaic of diplomatic maneuvers, humanitarian efforts, and public outcry. The situation underscored the intricate balance of geopolitics in the Middle East and the ongoing struggle for a lasting solution to the Israel-Palestine conflict. As the dust settled, the world watched with bated breath, hoping for a path towards enduring peace in a region long haunted by the specters of war and division.

CHAPTER 11: THE HUMANITARIAN AND CULTURAL IMPACT

The Refugee Crisis and Diaspora

The October 2023 conflict between Israel and Palestinian factions precipitated a profound refugee crisis, exacerbating an already complex diaspora situation. The intensity of the conflict forced countless families to flee their homes, seeking safety and shelter.

Escalating Displacement in Gaza The heavy bombardment and ground invasion in Gaza led to mass displacement. Thousands of Gazans found themselves homeless, with entire neighborhoods reduced to rubble. The UNRWA and other humanitarian organizations scrambled to provide temporary shelter in schools and public buildings, but these quickly became overcrowded, with limited access to essential services like clean water and sanitation.

Cross-border Movements With the closure of borders and the intense scrutiny of movements, Gazans seeking refuge outside the Strip faced immense challenges. Egypt's Rafah crossing, a crucial exit point, saw desperate scenes as families tried to escape the escalating violence. However, restrictions and stringent security measures meant that many were turned back, left to fend for themselves amidst the chaos.

Impact on the West Bank In the West Bank, there was an influx of internally displaced persons from Gaza, further straining resources in a region already dealing with its political and economic struggles. The Palestinian Authority, along with international aid agencies, struggled to provide adequate assistance to these new arrivals, many of whom had lost everything.

Global Diaspora Reactions The global Palestinian diaspora reacted with a mix of profound grief and heightened activism. Communities around the world organized protests, fundraising drives, and awareness campaigns. Social media became a tool for diaspora Palestinians to share their stories, galvanize support, and lobby international governments for action.

Host Countries and International Aid Neighboring countries, traditionally host to Palestinian refugees, faced renewed pressure. Jordan and Lebanon, already home to large Palestinian refugee populations, found their resources stretched thin. International aid efforts were ramped up, but the blockade and conflict made it challenging to deliver essential supplies.

Long-term Consequences The refugee crisis highlighted the long-term consequences of the conflict on civilian populations. Families were separated, with many children orphaned or left to navigate the complexities of refugee life. The psychological impact, particularly on young people, was profound, with many experiencing trauma and uncertainty about their future.

In conclusion, the refugee crisis resulting from the October 2023 conflict added another layer to the already complex Palestinian diaspora experience. It underscored the urgent need for a sustainable solution to the Israeli-Palestinian conflict, one that addresses the root causes of displacement and ensures the right of return and resettlement for Palestinian refugees. As a war correspondent, witnessing the human toll of this crisis was a sobering reminder of the enduring impact of conflict on innocent lives.

Human Rights Concerns and International Law

The October 2023 conflict between Israel and Palestinian factions raised significant human rights concerns and posed complex questions regarding international law. The severity and scale of the conflict drew widespread scrutiny from international human rights organizations, legal experts, and the global community.

Civilian Casualties and Humanitarian Impact
One of the most pressing concerns was the high number of civilian casualties. The indiscriminate nature of rocket attacks from Gaza into Israeli territories and the intensive Israeli bombardments in Gaza resulted in a tragic loss of life, including women and children. These incidents raised questions about adherence to the principles of distinction and

proportionality under international humanitarian law, which mandates the protection of civilians during armed conflicts.

Destruction of Civilian Infrastructure The conflict saw significant destruction of civilian infrastructure in Gaza, including homes, schools, hospitals, and water and sanitation facilities. This destruction not only caused immediate harm but also had long-term implications for the health and welfare of the population. The targeting of infrastructure essential for civilian life raised concerns about potential violations of the Geneva Conventions.

Use of Certain Weapons and Tactics Allegations surfaced about the use of certain types of weapons that could be considered illegal under international law. Reports of the use of white phosphorus and other incendiary devices, which cause severe burns and environmental damage, were particularly concerning.

Additionally, the tactics employed during the conflict, such as the reported use of human shields and the targeting of densely populated areas, were subjects of international condemnation.

Blockade and Access to Humanitarian Aid Israel's implementation of a siege on Gaza, restricting access to essential goods, medical supplies, and humanitarian aid, was a significant point of contention. This blockade exacerbated the humanitarian crisis and was considered by many as a form of collective punishment, which is prohibited under the Fourth Geneva Convention.

Treatment of Prisoners and Hostages The treatment of prisoners and hostages captured during the conflict was another area of concern. Reports of ill-treatment and lack of due process rights for detainees on both sides drew criticism from human rights groups, emphasizing the need for adherence to the

Third Geneva Convention, which provides protections for prisoners of war.

Refugee Rights and Displacement The massive displacement of civilians and the ensuing refugee crisis highlighted issues regarding the right to return and the protection of refugees. The forced displacement of populations and the destruction of homes without military necessity potentially violated international human rights laws and norms.

International Criminal Court (ICC) and War Crimes Investigations The International Criminal Court's involvement was a significant development, with calls for a thorough investigation into possible war crimes and crimes against humanity committed by both Israeli and Palestinian actors. The ICC's examination aimed to hold individuals accountable and bring justice to victims.

International Response and Legal Accountability The response of the international community was crucial in addressing these concerns. The United Nations, along with various human rights organizations, called for independent investigations into alleged violations of international law. They also urged both parties to respect international human rights and humanitarian laws and norms.

In summary, the October 2023 conflict not only resulted in immediate human and material losses but also posed significant challenges to international law and human rights norms. The pursuit of accountability and justice for the victims remained a critical issue in the conflict's aftermath, emphasizing the need for a comprehensive and just resolution to the long-standing Israeli-Palestinian conflict.

Cultural and Societal Impact on Both Sides

The October 2023 conflict between Israel and Palestinian factions had a profound cultural and societal impact on both sides, deeply affecting communities, altering perceptions, and influencing the social fabric in significant ways.

Trauma and Psychological Impact The conflict left deep psychological scars on both populations. In Gaza, the constant bombardment, loss of loved ones, and the fear of being targeted led to widespread trauma, especially among children who constitute a significant portion of the population. In Israel, the incessant rocket attacks from Gaza instilled a continuous state of fear and anxiety, disrupting daily life and leaving psychological impacts that would last long after the cessation of hostilities.

Impact on Art and Expression Culturally, the conflict influenced artistic expression on both sides. In Gaza, art became a medium to portray the suffering, resilience, and defiance of the people. Many artists used their work to document the destruction and human toll of the conflict, often as a form of protest and to draw international attention to their plight. In Israel, the conflict was reflected in music, literature, and cinema, with artists grappling with themes of security, moral dilemmas, and the continuous search for peace.

Shifts in Public Opinion and Political Discourse
The conflict led to shifts in public opinion and political discourse within both societies. In Israel, there was an increase in nationalistic sentiments and a hardening of attitudes toward the Palestinian issue. This shift influenced political dynamics, leading to a rise in support for more conservative and security-focused policies. Conversely, in Palestinian society, there was a surge in support for Hamas and other militant factions,

seen by many as defenders of Palestinian rights against Israeli aggression.

Community Solidarity and Resilience In the face of adversity, both societies witnessed remarkable displays of community solidarity and resilience. In Gaza, amidst the rubble of destroyed buildings, communities came together to support each other, sharing resources and providing emotional support. In Israel, communities in the most affected areas saw an outpouring of support from across the country, with volunteers and organizations providing aid and comfort to those in shelters or whose homes were damaged.

Diaspora Engagement and International Solidarity The conflict also had a significant impact on the global diaspora. Jewish and Palestinian diasporas around the world were actively engaged, often expressing solidarity with their respective sides.

This engagement was manifested in protests, advocacy, fundraising efforts, and a heightened sense of connection to their ancestral homelands.

Intergenerational Impact and Education The conflict's impact was also felt in the realm of education and intergenerational relations. In Palestinian society, the conflict became a part of the narrative passed down to younger generations, shaping their perceptions of identity and resistance. In Israel, the conflict influenced educational discussions around national history, security, and coexistence, with a focus on preparing younger generations for the complexities of the regional dynamics.

Social Media and Information Warfare The role of social media in shaping societal perceptions was significant. Both sides used social media platforms to disseminate information, rally support, and counter the narratives of the other side. This 'information warfare' played a crucial role in influencing public opinion and international perceptions of the conflict.

In conclusion, the October 2023 conflict between Israel and Palestine had a multifaceted impact on the societies of both regions. It influenced cultural expressions, altered political landscapes, and had a lasting effect on the collective psyche of the people, reinforcing the urgent need for a sustainable resolution to the long-standing conflict.

CHAPTER 12: ATTEMPTS AT PEACE AND FUTURE PROSPECTS

Historical Peace Efforts and Failures

Historical peace efforts between Israel and Palestine have been numerous, marked by both significant milestones and notable failures. These efforts, spanning several decades, reflect the complex and multifaceted nature of the conflict.

Camp David Accords (1978) The Camp David Accords, brokered by U.S. President Jimmy Carter between Israeli Prime Minister Menachem Begin and Egyptian President Anwar Sadat, were a landmark in Middle Eastern diplomacy. While it was an Egypt-Israel peace agreement, it laid groundwork for future peace efforts with the Palestinians, introducing frameworks for negotiating Palestinian autonomy.

Madrid Conference (1991) The Madrid Conference, convened by the U.S. and the Soviet Union following the Gulf War, marked the first time that Israeli, Palestinian, and Arab leaders came together for direct negotiations. The conference set the stage for subsequent bilateral talks, but direct Israeli-Palestinian issues remained largely unresolved.

Oslo Accords (1993-1995) The Oslo Accords, a series of agreements negotiated secretly in Norway, were a major breakthrough. The accords established the Palestinian Authority and set forth a process towards achieving a two-state solution. However, the failure to adequately address core issues like Jerusalem, settlements, refugees, and borders, as well as ongoing violence, ultimately hindered their full implementation.

Camp David Summit (2000) The Camp David Summit, hosted by U.S. President Bill Clinton, brought together Israeli Prime Minister Ehud Barak and Palestinian Leader Yasser Arafat. The summit saw significant negotiations over final status issues but ended without an agreement, partly due to disagreements over Jerusalem and refugees. The failure of the summit was followed by the outbreak of the Second Intifada.

Road Map for Peace (2003) The Road Map for Peace, proposed by the U.S., EU, UN, and Russia (the Quartet), outlined a phased approach to resolving the conflict. It included Palestinian statehood as the end goal but was hindered by mutual non-compliance and the escalation of violence.

Annapolis Conference (2007) The Annapolis Conference, initiated by U.S. President George W. Bush, aimed to relaunch the peace process. It resulted in a commitment to negotiations but failed to lead to significant progress, with issues like settlements and control of Jerusalem proving intractable.

Kerry's Peace Effort (2013-2014) U.S. Secretary of State John Kerry's intensive peace effort in 2013-2014 aimed to revive the stalled peace process. Despite numerous rounds of talks, the effort collapsed, with both sides blaming each other for the failure.

Trump's Peace Plan (2020) The Trump administration's Peace Plan, dubbed the "Deal of the Century," was heavily criticized for being biased towards Israel. It proposed a conditional pathway to a fragmented Palestinian state, but was outright rejected by the Palestinians and received little international support.

Abraham Accords (2020) While not a direct Israeli-Palestinian peace initiative, the Abraham Accords, brokered by the U.S. under the Trump administration, led to the normalization of relations between Israel and several Arab states. The accords shifted regional dynamics but were criticized for sidelining the Palestinian issue.

In summary, the history of peace efforts between Israel and Palestine is characterized by a cycle of high hopes and deep disappointments. The failure to fully address key issues and mutual mistrust continue to impede the path towards a lasting peace.

CONCLUSION

Reflections on the Long-Term Conflict

Reflecting on the long-term Israel-Palestine conflict, as a war reporter with decades of experience, I have observed a complex historical, political, and human elements that define this enduring struggle. The narrative of this conflict is not just a chronicle of wars and diplomacy, but a story of people, dreams, and relentless hope amidst despair.

Historical Roots and Enduring Narratives: The conflict's roots are deeply historical, intertwining the aspirations and tragedies of two peoples. The Jewish longing for a homeland, magnified by the horrors of the Holocaust, and the Palestinian quest for self-determination have been central narratives. Both sides carry narratives of displacement and suffering – the Nakba for Palestinians and the struggle for survival and security for Israelis.

Cycle of Violence and Hope: I've witnessed cycles of intense violence followed by periods of hope brought about by peace initiatives. Yet, each cycle leaves deeper scars, hardening attitudes and diminishing trust. The Oslo Accords, the Camp David Summit, and other efforts showed potential, but ultimately failed to bridge deep-seated mistrust and conflicting national aspirations.

Life in the Shadow of Conflict: Reporting from the ground, I've seen the everyday impact of the conflict. In Gaza, life under blockade is marked by economic hardship and the constant threat of conflict. In Israeli border towns, families live with the fear of rocket attacks. This perpetual state of tension shapes the psyche of both communities.

Changing Regional Dynamics: The shifting geopolitics of the Middle East, particularly the Abraham Accords, have altered regional dynamics. Traditional alliances have shifted, potentially sidelining the Palestinian issue while opening new diplomatic avenues for Israel.

The Human Cost: The most poignant aspect of this conflict is its human cost. I've spoken with families who lost loved ones, youths who have known nothing but conflict, and elders who recall times of peace and coexistence. The conflict's enduring legacy is a generation growing up in an environment of division and hostility.

The Role of Leadership and International Community: Leadership on both sides has often been driven by immediate political needs rather than long-term peace objectives. International efforts, while well-intentioned, have sometimes lacked a cohesive strategy, been influenced by global politics, or failed to address the core issues that fuel the conflict.

The Voice of Civil Society: Amidst political impasses, it's the voices of civil society – grassroots movements, NGOs, and individuals – that have continued to advocate for peace and reconciliation. Their efforts, often overlooked, are crucial in keeping the hope of coexistence alive.

Emerging Challenges and Technology: Modern challenges like social media's role in shaping perceptions, the proliferation of misinformation, and the impact of technology on warfare add new dimensions to the conflict.

The Path Forward: Looking ahead, the path to peace is fraught with complexities. It requires addressing historical grievances, security concerns, and the need for mutual recognition and respect. A solution must involve not just political agreements but a transformation in the hearts and minds of the people.

In conclusion, the Israel-Palestine conflict, with its deep historical roots and evolving nature, remains one of the most challenging and heart-wrenching issues of our time. The path to peace is uncertain, but the resilience of those who continue to strive for a better future offers a glimmer of hope in a landscape often overshadowed by despair.

The Path Forward: Possibilities and Uncertainties

In my years covering the Israel-Palestine conflict, the path forward has always been fraught with complexities and uncertainties. However, amidst the seemingly intractable nature of this conflict, possibilities for a resolution still exist, though they require concerted effort, compromise, and a fundamental shift in approach from all involved parties.

1. Mutual Recognition and Respect: A foundational step is mutual recognition and respect for each other's right to exist. This entails Israel recognizing the right of the Palestinian people to a sovereign state and Palestinians recognizing Israel's right to exist in security. This mutual acknowledgment is crucial for overcoming historical grievances and moving towards reconciliation.

2. Addressing Core Issues: Key issues such as borders, security, refugees, settlements, and the status of Jerusalem must be addressed comprehensively. These are not only political but also emotional issues, deeply tied to the identity and history of both peoples. Any viable solution must consider the realities on the ground and the aspirations of both sides.

3. International Involvement and Support: The international community plays a critical role. Effective diplomacy requires not just intermittent engagement but sustained and balanced involvement. International actors must be willing to exert pressure where needed while providing support for peace initiatives. This includes economic aid, security guarantees, and assistance in building institutions and infrastructure.

4. Empowering Moderates and Civil Society: Often, the voices of moderation are drowned out by extremists on both sides. Empowering moderate voices, including NGOs, community leaders, and civil society organizations, can help bridge divides. These groups can foster grassroots initiatives that promote understanding, coexistence, and reconciliation.

5. Economic Cooperation and Development: Economic interdependence can be a powerful tool for peace. Joint economic projects, increased trade, and cooperation in areas like technology, water, and energy can benefit both Israelis and Palestinians, creating a stake in maintaining peace and stability.

6. Education and Cultural Exchanges: Education systems and cultural exchanges play a pivotal role in shaping perceptions. Initiatives that promote a more balanced understanding of each other's narratives can help break down stereotypes and build empathy among the younger generations.

7. Leveraging New Regional Dynamics: The changing political landscape in the Middle East, especially the normalization of relations between Israel and several Arab states, could provide new opportunities for peace. These countries can exert influence and facilitate dialogue between Israelis and Palestinians.

8. Addressing the Humanitarian Situation in Gaza: Improving the dire humanitarian situation in Gaza is crucial. This requires easing the blockade while ensuring security concerns are addressed. A stable and prosperous Gaza is essential for any lasting peace.

9. Continuous International Vigilance: The international community must remain vigilant against actions that undermine peace efforts, such as settlement expansion, violence against civilians, and incitement.

10. Preparing for the Long Haul: Finally, it's important to recognize that peace is a long-term process. It requires patience, resilience, and a commitment to dialogue, even in the face of setbacks.

In summary, the path forward is not straightforward and is laden with challenges. Yet, the alternative – a perpetual cycle of violence and suffering – is a far grimmer prospect. The hope for peace lies in the courage to envision a different future, one where two peoples, with their rich histories and vibrant cultures, can coexist in peace and mutual respect.

APPENDIX

Chronology of Major Events

As a war reporter with decades of expericnce, I have witnessed the unfolding of the Israel-Palestine conflict, a complex events marked by intermittent periods of intense violence and tentative peace efforts. Here's a simplified chronology of the major events that have shaped this enduring conflict:

Late 19th Century: Emergence of Zionism and Palestinian nationalism in response to growing Jewish immigration to Palestine, then part of the Ottoman Empire.

1917: The Balfour Declaration by Britain supports a "national home for the Jewish people" in Palestine.

1920-1947: British Mandate in Palestine, seeing increased Jewish immigration and rising tensions with the Arab population.

1947: United Nations proposes partitioning Palestine into Jewish and Arab states. Jewish leaders accept, but Arab leaders reject the plan.

1948: State of Israel declared, leading to the first Arab-Israeli war. Hundreds of thousands of Palestinians become refugees. This event is celebrated in Israel as the War of Independence and mourned by Palestinians as the Nakba (Catastrophe).

1956: Suez Crisis, a brief war involving Egypt, Israel, Britain, and France, over control of the Suez Canal.

1967: Six-Day War. Israel captures the Gaza Strip, West Bank, East Jerusalem, the Golan Heights, and Sinai Peninsula. Start of Israeli occupation in these territories.

1973: Yom Kippur War. Egypt and Syria launch a surprise attack on Israel on the Jewish holy day of Yom Kippur.

1978: Camp David Accords, leading to a peace treaty between Egypt and Israel.

1987-1993: First Intifada (Palestinian uprising) against Israeli occupation.

1993: Oslo Accords signed, a major step towards resolving the conflict, though key issues remained unresolved.

2000-2005: Second Intifada erupts after failed peace talks, marked by intense violence.

2005: Israel disengages from the Gaza Strip, evacuating settlers and military.

2006: Hamas wins Palestinian elections and eventually seizes control of Gaza, leading to a split with the Fatah-controlled Palestinian Authority in the West Bank.

2008, 2012, 2014: Several conflicts between Israel and Hamas in Gaza, causing significant casualties and destruction.

2020: The Abraham Accords, normalization agreements between Israel and several Arab states, excluding the Palestinians.

May 2021: A severe escalation in violence following tensions in Jerusalem and an 11-day conflict between Israel and Hamas.

October 2023: The most severe and devastating conflict since the creation of Israel. Hamas launches a massive attack on Israeli territory, leading to a large-scale Israeli response and a humanitarian crisis in Gaza.

This timeline, while not exhaustive, captures key moments that have defined the contours of a conflict deeply rooted in historical, political, and cultural complexities. The path towards a peaceful resolution remains arduous, with each of these events leaving a lasting impact on the regional and global landscape.

Key Figures in the Conflict

Throughout the decades-long Israel-Palestine conflict, several key figures have emerged, influencing the course of events and shaping the political landscape of the region. Here's a look at some of these influential personalities:

David Ben-Gurion: Israel's primary founder and the first Prime Minister, he played a crucial role in the establishment of the State of Israel and its early years.

Yasser Arafat: As the long-time leader of the Palestine Liberation Organization (PLO), Arafat was a central figure in the Palestinian struggle, known for both his leadership in the conflict and his role in peace negotiations.

Golda Meir: The fourth Prime Minister of Israel, known for her leadership during the challenging times of the Yom Kippur War.

Anwar Sadat: The President of Egypt who made a historic visit to Israel in 1977, leading to the Camp David Accords and the Egypt-Israel Peace Treaty, the first of its kind between Israel and an Arab country.

Menachem Begin: Israeli Prime Minister who signed the peace treaty with Egypt, significantly altering the dynamic of the Middle Eastern conflict.

Yitzhak Rabin: As Prime Minister of Israel, he played a key role in the Oslo Accords, which was a major attempt at resolving the Israeli-Palestinian conflict. His assassination in 1995 was a significant blow to the peace process.

Mahmoud Abbas: The President of the Palestinian Authority and a key figure in peace negotiations, known for his more diplomatic approach compared to Arafat.

Benjamin Netanyahu: A dominant figure in Israeli politics, known for his hardline stance on security and his long tenure as Prime Minister.

Hamas Leaders (Ismail Haniyeh, Khaled Meshaal, Yahya Sinwar): Leaders of Hamas, the Islamist political and militant group controlling the Gaza Strip since 2007. They have been central to the conflict, particularly in the Gaza-Israel confrontations.

Ariel Sharon: Israeli general and politician, known for his controversial role in Lebanon and as the architect of Israel's disengagement from the Gaza Strip in 2005.

Ehud Barak: Israeli Prime Minister who participated in the Camp David Summit in 2000, an intensive but ultimately unsuccessful attempt to negotiate peace with the Palestinians.

Sheikh Ahmed Yassin: Founder and spiritual leader of Hamas, he was a prominent figure in the First and Second Intifadas.

Shimon Peres: A Nobel Peace Prize laureate, Peres served in several key positions in the Israeli government, including as Prime Minister and President. He was a pivotal figure in the Oslo Accords and a proponent of peace with the Palestinians.

Hanan Ashrawi: A prominent Palestinian leader and spokeswoman, particularly during the First Intifada and subsequent peace talks. She's been a strong advocate for Palestinian rights and a two-state solution.

Avigdor Lieberman: An influential Israeli politician known for his hardline views on security and the Palestinian issue, having served in key ministerial roles including as Israel's Defense Minister.

Marwan Barghouti: A leader in the First and Second Intifadas, Barghouti is a prominent figure in the Palestinian Fatah party. He's been imprisoned by Israel since 2002, but remains an influential figure in Palestinian politics.

Ehud Olmert: As Prime Minister of Israel, he was involved in extensive peace negotiations with the Palestinians, including the Annapolis Conference in 2007.

Saeb Erekat: A senior Palestinian negotiator and politician, Erekat was a key figure in peace talks with Israel for many years.

Tzipi Livni: An Israeli politician who played a significant role in peace negotiations with the Palestinians, serving as Israel's Foreign Minister and leading talks during the Annapolis Conference.

Hosni Mubarak: As the President of Egypt, he played a crucial role in mediating between Israel and the Palestinians, particularly after the Camp David Accords.

Jimmy Carter: The former U.S. President was instrumental in the Camp David Accords, which led to the first peace treaty between Israel and an Arab country (Egypt).

King Hussein of Jordan: His leadership led to the Israel-Jordan Peace Treaty in 1994, normalizing relations between the two countries.

Tony Blair: As the Quartet's special envoy, the former British Prime Minister was involved in efforts to facilitate the peace process between Israel and the Palestinians.

Bill Clinton: The former U.S. President hosted the Camp David Summit in 2000, a significant effort to negotiate peace between Israel and Palestine.

These individuals, among others, have left indelible marks on the history of the conflict. Their actions and decisions have had profound implications, not only for Israel and Palestine but for the broader Middle East and the international community.

Made in the USA
Columbia, SC
10 April 2024